Political Connection and Financial Fraud in China

Modern China Series

Political Connection and Financial Fraud in China

Peng Jinqian

North American Business Press

Political Connection and Financial Fraud

ISBN: 9781948915137

NORTH
AMERICAN BUSINESS
PRESS

North American Business Press
Atlanta, Georgia
Miami, Florida
New York, New York,
Toronto, Canada

FIRST PRINTING, 2019

About Modern China Series

China, as one of the oldest civilized regions in the world, has emerged as something of a "new world" because it is working to embrace its own essence and heritage and link them to viable economic strategies. In the last 25 years, China has made tremendous strides by doing so. The country and her people have every right to take pride in these accomplishments. With these successes under their belt, many Chinese leaders and intellectuals anticipate continuing growth. China's plans and strategies, furthermore, are often based upon this premise.

There is tremendous interest in the US on the Chinese economy and business environment. China has emerged as a global super power, and scholars and businessmen in the US are keenly interested in learning how this is going to continue to affect them and how they can do business with China. In response to growing interest from international and Asian scholars, North American Business Press is pleased to announce our Modern China Series (MCS) books, which is first of such series in the US and has garnered tremendous interest both in the US and around the world. With our first book reaching stores in September 2011, this initiative is aimed at developing relationships between NABP and Chinese scholars who desire to promote their academic and applied business writings to the rest of the world.

We have had overwhelming demand for the Modern China Series from both authors who would like to publish in the series and people who would like to read the books. Currently, there are ten books published in the series and, additionally, we have a couple of dozen books that we are considering for the series. The books have been viewed by tens of thousands of people from the U.S. and the rest of the world.

We have published books relating to several areas revolving around the Chinese business environment. We have a few that focus on the best practices in marketing in China; a couple relating to "best practices" in doing business in China; and a few on the outlook of the Chinese economy. The market for the Modern China Series is huge. There are tens of thousands of scholars that are keenly interested in the continued growth of the Chinese economy and the implications that will have on the business world. Even more significant are the millions of businessmen that are interested in the impact that China will continue to have on the global economy. It is difficult to pin down the exact demand for the series, but it Is very large.

We have big plans for growing the Moderns China Series. This has the potential to one of the most significant economic/business series ever produced. We are very selective with the books that we will add to the collection, but we encourage any scholars who think they have unique and interesting perspectives on China to submit their books to us. From the readers perspective, we are committed to producing high quality books on a regular basis so that readers should expect a steady stream of insightful books to be coming out for many years to come.

This initiative is headed by Dr. Robert Tian, a renowned researcher and academic, who spearheads our efforts in partnering with foreign authors and administering day-to-day operations of this series. Dr. Tian, a Vice-President with North American Business Press and Editor of this series, spends much of his time in Beijing, Shanghai, and other Chinese cities, focusing on developing and managing our interests with authors and universities. Below is the list for the books we have published:

Enterprise Strategy: New Horizon authored by Zhang Xiuyu
Governance of Private Enterprises in Modern China authored by Zhong Qin
The Art of War and Enterprise Strategy Management authored by Fu Shouzhi
Marketing Issues in Modern China edited by Robert Guang Tian et al.
The Footprints of the Academician authored by Fu Zhouzhi
Marketing and Economics in Modern China (I) edited by Xiaoguang Qi et al.
Marketing and Economics in Modern China (II) edited by Wang Tianjin et al.
An Islamic Heritage in China authored by Ma Zhanming
China Environmental Anthropology authored by Wang Tianjin, Tian Guang, and Ma Jianfu
Can China Rule the New World? Authored by Tian Guang and Chen Gang

Critiques on Pan-marketization authored by Li Cunlin, Liu Hongfei, and Tian Guang
Economic and Business Anthropology in China edited by Xiaoguang Qi and Tian Guang
China-Mongolia Economic Corridor authored by Eerdun Taoketao, Zhang Zhe, Wang Gang and Wei Lisi
Anthropology of Chinese Foodways authored by Tian Guang and Chen Gang
Urbanization of Rural China authored by Li Taohong
Political Connection and Financial Fraud in China by Peng Jinqian

Preface

Private enterprises have played a significant role in China's economic growth. However, financial frauds are often widespread among these private enterprises. My study aims to explore potential determinants of financial frauds in China. Guided by the prospect theory, I use the expectation level of firm performance as a reference point and investigate whether the pressure from failing to meet the performance benchmark would induce managers to engage in risky financial frauds. My sample includes 6903 firm-year observations for a period from 2007 to 2015. I use the CSMAR Database and manually code the financial fraud data.

My main findings support the predictions of the prospect theory that the past performance relative to industry expected performance affects the possibility of financial frauds. Furthermore, the positive effects of past performance pressure on financial frauds are stronger for firms with, 1) greater political connections, 2) higher financing constraints, and 3) more intensive industry competition. Finally, the institutional environment reduces the possibility of financial frauds.

My study contributes to the literature of financial frauds. I examine both behavioral factors (under the framework of prospect theory) and strategic considerations of political connections and financing constraints. This thesis integrates multiple factors of political capital and institutional environment into the framework of business behavior. This integration enhances our understanding of financial frauds in the context of China and has implications for academia, practitioners and policy makers.

Peng Jinqian

June 27, 2019

Acknowledgements

My three-year doctoral program is like a fleeting show; I thought it would be a long time, but I am about to graduate in a flash. Looking back on the three years in the Hong Kong Polytechnic University, I was learning from a number of elites, and got acquainted with the pillars of society, which would be an unforgettable memory in my life. Moreover, many people have cared, guided and helped me with my learning and growth.

My deepest gratitude goes first and foremost to Professor C.S. Agnes Cheng, my supervisor, for his careful guidance and patient instructions in all stages of the writing of the thesis. Professor Cheng has always encouraged me and given some advice and suggestions in time during the writing of the thesis. Moreover, he has always set aside time in his busy schedule to discuss with me on the path and direction to solve the problem in the writing of the thesis, as well as constantly encouraged me and given me the confidence to overcome difficulties. His strict requirements for this thesis have always given me an impetus to constantly strive for perfection and try my best to complete the thesis. After the completion of the first draft of the thesis, he also gave feedback on the detailed suggestions for revision, involving his warm care and careful guidance during the six rounds of revision. What's more, I have greatly admired him for his academic foundation and moral cultivation. It is an incredible honor for me to become a student of Professor Cheng.

Second, I would like to express my heartfelt gratitude to Professor Li Jiang, my supervisor, for his great assistance in the writing of the thesis. I remember that Professor Jiang not only patiently answered my questions in the learning of the core concept of prospect theory in the study of this thesis, but also helped me collect the cutting-edge research literature on this theory in international journals. During the writing of the thesis, I have discussed with Professor Jiang many times, and he answered my questions in a patient and meticulous way. Every time I discussed the thesis with him on WeChat, we would talk for more than one hour, and he would always expand my thinking, which has made me grateful and deeply moved.

I would also like to acknowledge my indebtedness to the teachers who have taught me the cutting-edge theoretical knowledge in this field, including Professor Wilson Tong, Professor Jiye Mao, Professor Xin Xu, Professor Jun Liu, Professor Wu Liu, Professor Hua Song, Professor Fang Gu and Professor Hongyan Yang, who have not only taught me the cutting-edge knowledge and the methods of learning theories, but also stimulated my pioneering thinking of learning, thus laying a good foundation for the writing of the thesis.

I am also grateful to all of my PhD classmates, including Dr. Qiang Li, Wenchao Bo, Xiaotong Zhang, Xianjin Xu, Renwei Zeng, Jun Zhong and Xiaoqi Chen, for their support and encouragement, which enriched my life during the PhD studies and left a deep memory.

Special thanks should go to my family members for their understanding and support of my decision and process to pursue a doctor's degree. Their understanding and support is the biggest pillar for me to successfully complete my studies. Over the past three years, I have spent too little time with them and care too little about them. But the family is the top priority in my mind. No matter how high and far I go, I will be together with them forever.

Finally, my gratitude also extends to Professor Haitian Lu in the Hong Kong Polytechnic University, Professor Shiheng Wang in the Hong Kong University of Science and Technology and Professor Ying Foon Chow, who have participated in the review and defense of my thesis, as well as all the teachers, colleagues and friends who have cared about and helped me.

Peng Jinqian

June 27, 2019

Foreword

Liang Yong Wan

On November 26, 1990, the Shanghai Stock Exchange, the first stock exchange in China, was established, which marked the beginning of the securities market in China. With the development and prosperity of the securities market, some negative phenomena arise accordingly, which can not be avoided in the development course of the securities market. After more than 20 years of continuous development, China's securities market is gradually becoming mature from its immature state, and gradually perfecting its supervision from the lack of supervisory measures, which has become an important component of China's national economy and has made significant contributions to boosting the growth of national economy. With the continuous improvement of economic level, the increasing strength of supervision, and the gradual enhancement of corporate governance, financial fraud has emerged in an endless stream among China's listed companies during the development stages of market economy, the proportion of companies violating regulations is much higher than that in western developed countries, and the ratio of companies committing severe violations has shown an upward trend, which not only exert a serious impact on investors' confidence in investing in China's capital market, but also hinder the healthy growth of capital market and listed companies. In the long run, its negative impact on China's economy will go beyond measure.

The financial fraud of listed companies has always been a hot topic in academic circles, and the two-factor, three-factor and four-factor theories of fraud explain the motives of financial fraud to a certain extent, but these theories are mostly based on the context of the West. However, in view of the special interests exchanges between the government and state-owned enterprises under the traditional institutional environment in China, the recognition of fraud by enterprises under the influence of relationship culture and the acquiescence of external regulators and other exceptional circumstances in China, the motives of fraud in China's listed companies tend to be complicated. In explaining financial fraud of listed companies in China, even the mature fraud triangle theory and

GONE theory have such evident problems as varied characteristics and insufficient explanatory power, which may be due to two reasons. One is that the motives of financial fraud may vary from each other under different circumstances, while the circumstances of China and the West are distinguished in few of the existing studies. The other is that the formation mechanism is seldom involved in relevant studies. In the formation process of financial fraud, there is a black box in the mechanism of fraud incentives, which is difficult to be further verified in the existing theory of fraud incentives. In addition, in various stages of fraud, there will also be some differences in the mechanism of fraud motive, while the existing research rarely explores the changes in the role of its inducing factors in different courses of fraud. In view of this, it will be of great significance to base itself on the Chinese circumstances to find a more effective interpretive structure to identify the motives of financial fraud and to explore its mechanism of financial fraud in various stages of fraud.

Under this background, Dr. Peng Jinqian, based on his first-line insight into the capital market in China and his solid academic research foundation, conducted a penetrating analysis of financial fraud of listed companies in China by combining the latest research progress of prospect theory. On the basis of institutional theory, the book introduces the level of performance expectation in prospect theory as a reference point for financial fraud decision-making of enterprises, analyses and tests whether listed companies will choose to engage in financial fraud under the double pressure of historical expected performance and industry expected performance, as well as how organizations and external resources promote or suppress the financial fraud of listed companies, and finally draws a conclusion of great theoretical and practical value, which is of great significance for deepening the institutional reform of China's capital market and giving effective impetus to the market supervision mechanism at the current stage.

As the author said, some viewpoints in the book need to be further deliberated, but overall, it is a pioneering work with broad vision, rigorous structure and novel ideas.

Table of Contents

Chapter 1 Introduction

This chapter mainly consists of three parts. Firstly, the first three sections mainly introduce the research background of this book, including the realistic background and theoretical background, and on this basis, sort out the research problems of this book. Secondly, the fourth section briefly elaborates on the logical thinking to solve these research problems and gives a brief introduction to the research methods to be used in this book. Finally, the fifth and sixth sections briefly introduce the major research concepts of this book and list its main framework.

Realistic Background

Since the establishment of Shanghai Stock Exchange in 1990, China's capital market has been established for more than 20 years. By the end of 2016, the number of listed companies had grown from 10 at first to 3,337, with a total market value of 50.62 trillion Yuan and a circulation market value of 39.29 trillion Yuan, 127 times and 407 times higher than the total market value of 396 billion Yuan and the circulation market value of 96.4 billion Yuan in 1994 respectively (Liu, 2016; Wang, 2014). In 2016, the total market value of listed companies accounted for 68.04% of Gross National Product (GNP), which reflects that capital market plays a decisive role in China's economic take-off. However, in spite of some positive effects, the development of the securities market has always been accompanied by the irregularities of listed companies as a ghost. A number of financial fraud incidents have occurred in China, including the earliest incident of Hongguang Industry Co., Ltd. (Hongguang Incident) and incident of Hainan Minyuan Modern Agriculture Development Co.,Ltd. (Qiongminyuan Incident), the false financial statements of Guangxia (Yinchuan) Industry Co., Ltd. in 2001(hereinafter referred to as Yinguangxia Incident), the fabrication performance myth of Lantian Co., Ltd. in 2002 (hereinafter referred to as Lantian Incident), and the fraudulent listing of Yunnan Yuntou Ecology And Environment Technology Co.,Ltd. in 2010 (hereinafter referred to as Lvdadi Incident), and financial fraud of Wanfu Biotechnology(Hunan) Agricultural Development Co.,Ltd. in 2012 (hereinafter referred to as

Wanfushengke Incident), as well as the incidents of Aeolus Tyre Co., Ltd. and Jiangsu Sainty Marine Co., Ltd. in 2015 (hereinafter referred to as Aeolus Tyre Incident and Sainty Marine Incident,respectively), which have been greatly affecting the investors.

Table 1-1 List of the Most Representative Financial Fraud Incidents in China

Time of Disclosure	**Incident**	**Amount Involved (Unit: Yuan)**	**Consequences**
1998	Qiongminyuan Incident	566,000,000	Qiongminyuan Incident, as an enterprise fraud event, is the most representative since the establishment of China's securities market. After the incident, Hainan Minyuan Modern Agriculture Development Co., Ltd. was reorganized by its parent company and its stock name changed to Zhongguancun. The social shareholders of the Company were compensated by means of equal equity swap in the form of the equity of the new company. However, more than 500 corporate shareholders with a shareholding ratio of 20.96% were not compensated. In addition, the loss of state-owned assets was not announced.
1998	Hongguang Incident	200,000,000	It was called the first Incident of minority shareholders suing the listed company, which led to a large number of minority shareholders' struggle for rights protection for more than 10 years.
2001	Yinguangxia Incident	745,000,000	It was listed again thirteen years after being restructured.
2002	Lantian Incident	2,000,000,000	It resulted in the fall of Sun Heling, former director of Finance Department the Ministry of Agriculture.
2010	Lvdadi Incident	296,000,000	It was merged and restructured.

Time of Disclosure	Incident	Amount Involved (Unit: Yuan)	Consequences
2012	Wanfusheng ke Incident	740,000,000	It was sold to Legend Holdings Corporation.
2015	Aeolus Tyre Incident	Unknown	Its share price slumped.
2015	Sainty Marine Incident	200,000,000	It completely withdrew from the shipbuilding industry.
2016	Xintai Electric Incident	Unknown	It was delisted.

Data source: It was manually reorganized by the author.

With the continuous improvement of the economic level, increasing efforts have been made for supervision and the standard of corporate governance has been gradually enhanced accordingly. However, in the different stages of the development of market economy, the listed companies in China have committed financial frauds in an endless stream, and the proportion of violations is much higher than that of western developed countries, and the proportion of companies seriously violating regulations is also on the rise, which have not only greatly affected investors' confidence in investing in China's capital market, but also hindered the healthy growth of capital market and listed companies. In the long run, it will exert an inestimable negative impact on China's economy.

For these reasons, managers' financial frauds, such as fraudulent business volume, false declaration of asset value, and concealment of substantive information, are receiving increasing attention (Eaglesham & Rapoport, 2015). Therefore, the importance of financial fraud prediction and prevention has also become an important research topic that deeply attracts the attention of scholars in the field of governance. For a long time, securities regulatory authorities in various countries have tried every way possible to eradicate financial fraud, constantly improve the systems and strengthen supervision, but they are still caught in the cycle that the law is strong but the outlaws are ten times stronger. Even in the United States with the most perfect market supervision and system, the largest tides of frauds, represented by the Enron Incident, broke out at the beginning of the 21st century, which once again sounded the alarm to the regulatory and governance departments. At present, the securities regulatory authorities mainly deal with financial frauds by means of intensifying the punishment of violations. But even under the threat of various methods of severe punishment, a number of listed companies still challenge the law personally one after another. It can be seen that the governance of financial frauds is such an extremely complex domain that needs to be further analyzed. The forms and methods of financial fraud are changing with each passing day, which also reflects that there may be some deep-seated reasons for financial frauds of enterprises that can not be explained by the existing theory, so that it is necessary to have a more systematic understanding. This study will try to explain the causes of financial fraud from a new theoretical perspective and then put forward corresponding suggestions for the governance of financial fraud.

Under the background of globalization of economic development and gradual completion of China's reform of non-tradable shares, institutional environment, political connection and enterprise ownership related to the institutions are bound to attract wide attention from all walks of life, in order to further deepen the reform of institutional environment of modern enterprises in China. As the practice of reform and opening-up has lasted for nearly 30 years, the reality shows the listed companies in China based on state-owned shares present a situation of low efficiency, serious losses and declining performance on the whole, when a majority of enterprises are restructured and listed and formally go in line with modern companies, accompanied by the manipulation of the market, abuse of the funds raised, accounting fraud and other acts that encroach on the rights and interests of stakeholders, which enable us to pay attention to the fact that it is far from enough to construct a framework that meets the basic requirements of modern enterprise system, and to be more concerned about how to establish a complete set of mechanisms for supervision, checking and balancing on the basis of a series of rights restraint systems. For this reason, it has become an inevitable choice to improve the overall efficiency of listed companies in China by probing into the solutions to financial frauds under the framework of the systems.

Theoretical Background

Financial fraud is a fraudulent act by managers against investors and key stakeholders (Gande and Lewis, 2009; Shi et al., 2016). In the process, it is usually involved in corruption, concealment of the truth, distortion of performance information and concealment of systematic problems (Baucus & Near, 1991). Managers who engage in fraudulent practices can benefit from such practices, such as obtaining higher performance pay by falsifying the presentation of performance improvement, which has caused serious harm to the market reputation, investor confidence and enterprise value of enterprises(Geiger and North, 2006), and even led to managers thrown into jail (Beasley, 1996; Jaggi, 1975). Over the years, scholars have put a lot of efforts to uncovering the mystery of financial fraud.

In the previous documents, the causes of financial fraud and its governance mechanism have been explored in an all-round way (Kong & Yu, 2015), from the perspectives of the motivation theory (Beasley, 1996; Dyck & Zingales, 2003; Geiger & North, 2006; Jaggi, 1975), social psychology theory (Katz & Kahn, 1978; Robinson et al., 2012), neoinstitutional economic theory (Coase, 1998; Fich & Shivdasani, 2007), game theory (Dooley, 2002; Wilks & Zimbelman, 2004) and prospect theory (Cyert & March, 1963; Dyck et al., 2010; Harris & Bromiley, 2007). Among them, the studies based on the motivation theory, social psychology theory and neoinstitutional economic theory involve varied focuses, but generally speaking, they all aim to extract the correlation between various antecedent variables and financial fraud acts through the analysis of a large number of fraudulent acts. However, through such an analysis method, it is impossible to put forward a set of basic action framework of the people engaged in fraudulent acts, and to summarize and synthesize the systematic relationship among various antecedents. Therefore, the antecedents extracted from these theories are merely necessary but not sufficient conditions for financial fraud, while it is less likely to explain the causes of financial fraud in essence (Harris & Bromiley, 2007). The basic behavioral criteria of financial fraud actors are made clear in the game theory, as the cost-benefit analysis, to a certain extent, provides a comprehensive framework for the systematic mechanism of interaction between various influencing factors. However, game theory is based on the hypothesis of a completely rational man, which is difficult to satisfy in the real environment, and thus it is less likely to explain the deep-seated causes of financial frauds. At present, the most cutting-edge analysis of financial fraud research in academic circles comes from the analysis of prospect theory from the perspective of behavioral economics. On the basis of the thoughts of neo-classical economics, prospect theory revises the standard hypothesis of rational man, incorporates psychological factors into the cost-benefit analysis of corporate behavior, which will make up for the deficiencies of other theoretical perspectives in an effective way.

From the perspective of prospect theory (Kahneman & Tversky, 1979), financial fraud is an act of strategic change (Kang, 2008). The adaptability of enterprises to environmental changes exerts an extremely significant impact on their survival and development. Strategic adjustment, as a crucial strategy to cope with changes in the external environment, has been widely concerned by the theoretical circles. The extent to which an enterprise can make strategic adjustments, to a large extent, depends on the links between the organization and the environment (Burgelman, 1991), resources and capabilities (Cui et al., 2011), the characteristics of senior management in the organization (Boeker, 1997), mutual support between the middle-level management and the grass-roots employees (Sonenshein & Dholakia, 2012), the characteristics of the board of directors (Haynes & Hillman, 2010), performance in the earlier stage (Meyer et al., 1993), as well as media attention (Bednar et al., 2013). Throughout these studies, it is not difficult to find that the decision model of decision makers is an important approach to obtain knowledge about the behavior of strategic change.

Furthermore, prospect theory believes that the enterprise is a goal-oriented system, which adopts some simple decision rules to adjust the enterprise behavior based on performance feedback. Performance feedback provides a preliminary criterion for decision makers to assess the current performance of the enterprise, to determine whether alternative solutions are sought and whether changes in the existing operating rules of the enterprise are needed (Greve, 1998). Therefore, it is not difficult to understand that the performance goal of an enterprise is an important factor affecting the strategic behavior of decision makers.

Different from the traditional studies on strategic adjustment, which regards maximization of earnings or profits as the main decision-making goal of an enterprise, prospect theory holds that it is difficult for decision makers with bounded rationality to make maximized decisions and that the basis for their decisions is formed by comparing the actual situation with the expected reference points. For enterprises, the main decision-making reference point is the expected level of operation. That is to say, the decision-making of enterprises in the next stage will be based on the gap between the actual performance and the expected level of the current period. In case that the actual performance is lower than the expected level, the enterprise will define such state below expectation as a state of loss. When the actual performance is higher than the expected level, the enterprise will define the state above expectation as a state of gain. Based on these two distinct operating conditions, the decision makers will adopt entirely different decision-making behaviors (Cyert & March, 1963).

However, current studies on prospect theory mainly focus on how the gap between the actual performance and the expected level mentioned above affects positive risk-taking activities such as R&D (Bolton, 1993; Bowman, 1982; Bromiley, 1991; Grinyer & McKiernan, 1990), product and market strategies (Greve, 2003; Grinyer & McKiernan, 1990) and financial cost (Hadley et al., 1996; D'Aunno & Sutton, 1992). Moreover, one of the presuppositions implicit in these scholars' definition of risk-taking behavior is that entrepreneurs are mostly positive and have stronger ethical conduct, so that they will tend to take positive, legitimate or legitimate risk-taking behavior to improve the situation in case of the performance lower than the expectations, while they neglect that these entrepreneurs may also solve the difficulties in their businesses by means of negative, improper or even illegal risk-taking behavior. In fact, since the reform and opening up, China's rapid economic growth has been accompanied by negative risk-taking behavior, among which financial fraud is one of the worst cases. In view of this, we should not turn a blind eye to it.

The main contributions of this book are manifested in the following three aspects:

First of all, the strategic change of enterprises is divided into compliant change and illegal change, and the relationship between them and financial fraud acts is explored from the perspective of illegal change which has attracted less attention in traditional methods, so as to expand the framework of previous research on prospect theory and the decision-making of enterprises for risk taking, thereby enabling the theory to be more consistent with the characteristics of enterprises' risk-taking behavior in reality.

Second, most of the previous studies are based on the situation in the West while few studies are carried out based on the situation in China. Among the studies based on the West, more attention is paid to the analysis of the regulation mechanism of the resource status within the organization towards the relationship between the expectation gap and risk-taking behavior (Audia & Greve, 2006; Greve, 2011). However, based on the special background of China's transition economy, this book constructs a more complete context dependence model of risk-taking decision-making from the micro level of resources of the organization and the macro level of social institutional environment, which is to take into account the resource status within the organization and the characteristics of its external industry environment and other traditional contextual factors to analyze how these factors affect the choice of the enterprise on financial fraud acts under the condition of business expectation gap, pursuant to the characteristics of the institutional background of China's transition economy outside the enterprise. This study provides a new evidence and explanation for the context dependence model of enterprises' risk-taking decision-making. Especially, it provides a new perspective and evidence for revealing the shaping and restraining effects of institutional factors on risk-taking decision-making in the context of transition economy in China.

Third, although previous studies have demonstrated that there is a positive impact between the operating performance in the earlier stage and financial frauds, more of these studies focus on the motivation of financial fraud from the perspective of individual characteristics and psychological factors of decision makers, while ignoring the impact of institutions and related factors on managers' freedom in decision making (Lian et al., 2014; Lian et al., 2016).

In a word, the main contribution of this book is to establish a systematic framework for motivation analysis of strategic adjustment, which not only expands the motivation study of strategic adjustment, but also seeks for an excellent theoretical situation for the application of prospect theory. In particular, this book incorporates contextual factors such as characteristics of senior management and resource endowment into the performance feedback model of behavior decision-making in enterprises, which makes up for the shortcomings of previous studies that laid too much stress on the direct influence mechanism between performance expectation gap and decision-making behavior, but less stress on the deficiencies of contextual factors. It plays a positive role in the construction and improvement of performance feedback theory and prospect theory.

Research Questions

Prospect theory attaches great importance to the performance evaluation, opportunity search and decision-making mechanisms of the organizations, especially to how these processes ultimately affect the strategic decision-making of the organizations (Greve, 2003; Greve, 2003; Cyert & March, 1963; March, 1991). For this reason, the decision model based on performance feedback well includes the above contents (Greve, 2003; Greve, 2003), which holds that the behavior decisions of the organization in the next stage will be made by assessing the gap between the actual performance and the target expectations in the current period. When the actual performance is lower than the target expectation, the decision maker will define the state lower than the target expectation as a state of loss (March & Simon, 1958). Such dilemma of failure will drive enterprises to adopt risk-taking behaviors that are different from the previous inertial behavior in order to enable the organizational performance to return to a reasonable level of expectation (Cyert & March, 1963).

The risk-taking decision-making behavior of enterprises may be positive and legitimate, such as technological innovation, product or service improvement, management mechanism optimization, etc. (Bhaskaran, 2006), or it may be negative and destructive, such as financial fraud, rent seeking, illegal operation and so forth. Data estimates show that in real business activities, negative business practices are very common in the industry (Baumol, 1990). Since the reform and opening up, a number of immoral behaviors, such as financial fraud, tax evasion, corruption and bribery, tunneling from major shareholders and related party transactions, have always been accompanied by the development of market economy.

According to prospect theory, enterprises ultimately choose to adopt positive or negative coping strategies in the face of an expectation gap and make decisions mainly by means of cost-benefit analysis. In case that the return of negative risk-taking behavior is higher than the perceived potential risk, negative speculation will be adopted (Braithwaite, 1985; Coleman, 1987; Harris & Bromiley, 2007). In particular, when the actual performance is the performance is far below the expected level, it is often difficult for enterprises to improve their performance in a short time due to serious systemic problems, and thus there are hardly any legitimate ways to enable the performance to quickly return to the expected level. Under this state, the probability of the occurrence of low-cost illegal risk-taking behavior, which makes the financial performance of the enterprise improved in a short time, may also be greatly increased.

To sum up, even when the enterprises are under the state that their performance is below the expected level, there are other contextual factors that affect the choice of financial fraud by enterprises. That is to say, although financial fraud can quickly reverse the negative effects arising from poor performance, decision makers will still give up taking such actions from the perspective of cost-benefit analysis, in case of a too high risk of implementing financial fraud. As a result, factors that can influence decision makers' perception of the cost and benefits of negative risk-taking behavior are likely to be the key to curbing financial fraud. A large number of factors that play such a role arise in the existing literature, such as institutional environment, competitive status, industry culture, organizational characteristics and individual characteristics of entrepreneurs (Courtney, 2001; Giaccotto et al., 2005; Gunther-McGrath & Nerkar, 2004).

This book holds that institutional factors are a crucial and distinctive category among the numerous external contextual factors for China in the transition period, and the regional institutional disparity formed in the gradual market reform in China exerts a particularly significant impact on China's capital market. After the Great Depression from 1929 to 1933, the United States passed many laws, regulations and ordinances on stock trading, making it one of the most stringent countries in the world to regulate securities trading. At present, the two laws that play a fundamental role in regulating the stock market in the United States are Securities Act of 1933 and Securities Exchange Act of 1934. In addition, there are a number of regulations, such as Public Utility Holding Company Act of 1935, Investment Company Act of 1940 and Investment Advisers Act of 1940. Under the complete legal system, the supervision of various regulators is mainly achieved by legal means, while their actions are not arbitrary. Because of a set of strict punishment systems, securities traders and listed companies cover a high cost of violating regulations, as they tend to ultimately go bankrupt and lose all standing and reputation once they are involved in civil lawsuits because of irregular actions.

In contrast, the current nominal supervision pattern of the stock market in China integrates centralized and unified supervision and industry self-regulation. In fact, due to the lack of effective means of self-regulation and the imperfect supervision system in the Securities Industry Association, its self-regulation tends to be weak and feeble. However, the stock exchange should accept the unified supervision and leadership of the Securities Regulatory Commission, while its function of self-regulation has existed in name only. It is only a technical support system for the listing of stocks. Therefore, the regulatory power of China's securities market is concentrated in the government's supervisory department, while there are quite obvious administrative characteristics of the stock market supervision. The formulation of laws and regulations depends more on the will of the government than on the requirements of the market. Laws and regulations are promulgated hastily, frequently and mostly aimed to interfere with the operation of the stock market, which is not conducive to the objective and healthy development of the market. The governance of the stock market based on the laws, policies and regulations issued at any time leads to the phenomenon of policy market, which often causes the stock market to deviate from the fluctuation of the market, thus going against the healthy operation of the stock market. It is precisely because of the unique institutional environment different from foreign countries that institutional environment is an important and unavailable key element in the study of financial frauds of listed companies in China.

From the institutional point of view, the government background and external institutional environment of enterprises are important situational variables influencing the relationship between earnings pressure and financial fraud of listed companies. The cost-benefit analysis of earnings pressure on organizational financial fraud, on the one hand, depends on the background of government relations owned by the enterprise, because political capital will play a role in sheltering its irregularities. On the other hand, it also depends on the institutional environment factors, such as the legal system, the efforts of supervision and the degree of market-oriented operations in the region, because institutional environment will have a constraint effect on the violations. On this basis, this book mainly discusses the following questions pursuant to the dual mechanism of shelter and constraint:

First, how will the historical performance pressures and industry performance pressures of the enterprise affect its financial frauds?

Second, does political capital have a shelter effect on the financial frauds? How does it work?

Third, how will the abundance of organizational resources and industry competition affect the relationship between performance pressure and financial fraud of enterprises?

Fourth, do the normative nature of the institution and the efficiency of its implementation have a constraint effect on financial fraud? How does it work?

Logical Thinking and Research Methods

In view of the above research questions, this book follows the following ways of logical thinking through the stages of research design. First of all, the core issue of this book is financial fraud, so the relevant research of financial fraud is first combed in an all-round way. Second, the core analytical framework that affects financial fraud is explored according to the existing research conclusions and enlightenment, and a theoretical basis for the definition of related concepts is established. Third, the regulatory mechanism between performance pressure and financial fraud is taken into account from the perspective of institution based on the dual mechanism of shelter and constraint between political connection and institutional efficiency and the balancing effect of the shelter and constraint mechanism on financial fraud is studied. Based on the analysis of financial fraud, this book introduces the view of prospect theory and inquires into the causes of financial fraud and related governance mechanisms by combining the institutional analysis, and then constructs the basic theoretical framework and puts forward the corresponding research hypothesis.

In order to test whether the research hypothesis proposed in this book can be supported by real data, this book adopts empirical research method, which combines theoretical analysis and empirical test, and then carries out an empirical test of the research hypothesis proposed by means of theoretical building by collecting samples of listed companies and designing measurement scales. In terms of sample selection, the listed companies of Shanghai and Shenzhen A-share markets in China are the samples. The samples are selected and the data is mined in accordance with the announcement information of each sample company's IPO (public prospectus), the information on its home page and its annual reports so as to further measure the two key concepts of internal resources and external relations of the start-ups. The descriptive statistical analysis of related variables and hypothesis test of theoretical model are carried out according to the collated data. Finally, the results are summarized and analyzed.

Definition of Major Concepts

Financial Fraud

Fraud

The definition of fraud in Chinese and Western dictionaries has a long history, which shows that fraud is a common phenomenon that exists in human society for a long time. Among them, fraud is defined as the crime of getting money by deceiving people in Cambridge Dictionary. It is interpreted as wrongful or criminal deception intended to result in financial or personal gain in Oxford Dictionary. It is defined in detail in Longman Dictionary as the crime of deceiving people in order to gain something such as money or goods. In Collins Dictionary, it is defined relatively abstractly and the target of fraud is not directly defined as financial gain, but fraud is defined as the crime of gaining money or financial benefits by a trick or by lying. In China, fraud is also defined in the Modern Chinese Dictionary as a violation of law or discipline that is carried out by means of deception (Dictionary Editorial Office, Institute of Linguistics, Chinese Academy of Social Sciences, 2003). By summarizing the above viewpoints, it can be found that, despite numerous definitions, all of them emphasize the two features of fraud. Firstly, the implementer intends to deceive. Secondly, its fraudulent act goes against laws and regulations.

Corporate Fraud

Corporate fraud is one of the most concerned fields of fraud research with the most abundant related research findings. It is a collection of violations and illegal acts (O'Gara, 2004), where the actor gains benefits and damages the interests of others through intentional and illegal fraudulent acts. In terms of motivation, the chief objective of corporate fraud is to seek profits. As far as the scope of the actors is concerned, the actors of fraud may come from within the organization, such as company executives and employees, or from outside the organization, such as consumers. In light of this, corporate fraud may be either an act of insiders damaging the interests of the organization, such as asset tunneling embezzlement and bribery, or an act of insiders protecting the interests of the organization, such as temporarily surviving a crisis through falsification of financial reports, or an act of outsiders damaging the interests of the organization, such as credit card fraud. In recent years, with the continuous development of capital market, fraudulent financial reporting has gradually become one of the main forms of corporate fraud.

Financial Fraud, Fraudulent Financial Reporting and Accounting Fraud

Financial fraud refers to the practice that the members of an organization adopt illegal means such as financial fraud to seek their own benefits by intentionally harming the interests of others (Rezaee, 2002). In terms of the means of financial fraud, it can be divided into two categories: embezzlement of assets and fraudulent financial reporting. The former refers to the behavior that the members of an organization use illegal means such as financial fraud to damage the interests of the organization in order to seek their own interests, while the latter refers to the behavior that the management deliberately submits wrong or false accounting information in violation of accounting norms (Yang et al., 2009). False statements in financial fraud may involve all the financial information of the company, which is concerned by market participants and related to the investment decisions, while such statements are usually disseminated in the form of speeches, brochures, financial reports and financial evaluations.

Accounting fraud refers to the deliberate fraudulent acts by which the management of an enterprise seeks their own interests from the damage to the interests of the shareholders and creditors and other stakeholders by providing misleading financial reports (Elliott & Willingham, 1980), which makes it clear that the implementers of accounting fraud are company managers rather than ordinary employees, that the carriers of implementation are the company's financial reports, and that the economic consequences are to damage the interests of shareholders and creditors and other stakeholders. From the point of view of motivation, the implementer commits fraud in a subjective and intentional way, rather than an accidental or negligent way.

Fraudulent financial reporting, which was formally defined in the Report of the National Commission on Fraudulent Financial Reporting issued by the Committee of Sponsoring Organizations of the Treadway Commission (COSO) in 1987, refers to the practice that a company intentionally or indiscriminately provides false or misleading financial information with significant omissions in its external financial reports, which has a substantially negative impact on investors' decision-making. In the definition, the accounting errors of the company caused by its imprudent operation, which is broader than the general definition of accounting fraud. In addition, Association of Certified Fraud Examiners (ACFE) also explains the definition of fraudulent financial reporting, which lays stress on the subjective intent of fraudsters. Moreover, they believe that accounting fraud is the act of deliberately or intentionally misreporting or omission of facts, or that of directly providing misleading information, which results in the reader obtaining accounting information conducive to the judgment or decision-making of the fraudster.

In summary, the concepts of financial fraud, accounting fraud and fraudulent financial reporting have very similar connotations in practice. In practical research, the three are often mixed up. In spite of some differences, the three are mixed in the process of sampling and analysis as the samples in this book mainly come from the annual reports of listed companies, which will not affect the empirical results of this book. Therefore, they will be no longer distinguished in the following reviews. In this book, the author adopts the definition of financial fraud by Rezaee (2002) that financial fraud refers to the practice that the members of an organization use financial fraud and other illegal means to seek their own interests by intentionally damaging the interests of others.

Performance Pressure

The research on performance pressure first appeared in the book by Stein (1989) on the effectiveness of capital market. As an important research field of earnings management, performance pressure has attracted great attention from many scholars. For example, Baginski et al. (2002) and Cheng et al. (2005) discussed performance pressure and violations by senior executives. The early research on performance pressures of enterprises was mainly carried out from the perspective of corporate finance, and the researchers hold that the principal-agent issue arising from the governance of modern companies determines that the market evaluation of corporate performance is a key source of performance pressure for managers, which will affect their decision-making (Cheng et al., 2005). Earnings expectations of analysts, as a significant external mechanism of listed companies, can be regarded as the performance pressure of corporate management, which is of great significance to understand the governance of listed companies. In recent years, there have been an increasing number of studies on performance pressures (Zhang & Gimeno, 2016). For example, Xu Nianhang et al. (2012) studied the impact of analyst independence on earnings management of the enterprises, and pointed out that the more independent the analysts are, the more prominent their role in restraining earnings management will be, and the more significant their impact on positive earnings management will be.

However, with the interdisciplinary study of corporate governance, especially the deepening of the research on behavior decision-making based on behavioral finance and social psychology, a growing number of researchers believe that the earnings expectation of analysts as a measure of managers' performance pressure is not a fair or appropriate variable, especially in the developing countries where the market system is less perfect (Dhaliwal et al., 2012; He et al., 2016). On the one hand, the accuracy and validity of the measurement of earnings expectations by analysts depends on the trust of investors in the capital market to their results, but due to the incompleteness of market system, the predictions of analysts are vulnerable to the manipulation by stakeholders in countries with economies in transition, and the results are less credible for investors in the market (Ye et al., 2008). On the other hand, in the analyst market, there are a variety of predictions for the earnings of the same enterprise by several analysts, and even there is a huge gap between the results. For managers, the forecast results of analysts can not influence their decisions in an effective way.

In contrast, the prospect theory holds that the performance pressures of enterprises mainly come from two aspects: the performance level before the organization and the performance of the competitive organizations (Cyert & March, 1963), namely, the historical performance of the enterprise and industry performance (Moussetis, 2011). For both owners and managers of enterprises, the comparison of these two dimensions can reflect the performance of enterprises more intuitively and accurately than the predictions of analysts, and thus can influence the decision-making of managers to a greater extent (Chen & Miller, 2007). As far as managers are concerned, performance pressure will arise when the performance fails to achieve the expected level compared with the historical performance and industry performance, which will lead to problem-seeking behavior of the enterprise and even organizational change. When performance is higher than the expected level, the enterprise will be more willing to maintain the status quo (Cyert & March, 1963). In this study, the author mainly measures the impact of enterprises' performance pressure on managers' behavior decision-making by two dimensions of historical performance and industry performance.

Political Connection

Fisman (2001) first proposed the concept of political connection as the close personal relationship between enterprises and individuals with political authority. Due to the defects of the system and the fierce market competition, enterprises are motivated to establish and maintain good relations with the officials or departments of the government, which will enable such enterprises to create advantages in the process of competition (Krueger, 1974).

Fisman (2001) understood political connection as the personal relationship between enterprises and government officials, which tends to be so secret that it is less likely to collect related data for research. For this reason, subsequent scholars have made constant attempts to explore political connection from the perspective of other proxy variables. Bertr & et al. (2004) tried to define political connection from the perspective of CEO's academic structure and work experience. He believed that if the CEO of an enterprise graduated from an elite school which teemed with government officials used to work in a government department, it would be possible for the enterprise to establish political connection. Khwaja & Mian (2005) and Goldman et al. (2013) agree that political donation is likely to be a means for an enterprise to establish political connection with officials of the government, as the enterprise offers financial support to the political election of an official and the official is likely to provide the enterprise with some convenience within their own power after he is elected. However, the above definitions have some limitations. Faccio (2006) made up for the shortcoming from a more comprehensive perspective, believing that if the major shareholders or executives of an enterprise were members of the Congress, ministers, regional leaders, or had close ties with politicians in real power, the enterprise could be deemed to have political connection. The viewpoint has been widely adopted by foreign literatures due to its comprehensiveness and practicality (Feng et al., 2012).

China and the western developed countries are entirely different in political system. As China is developing at a high rate, its institutional building is far less perfect than that of the developed countries in the west. Political connection plays a very characteristic role in Chinese culture. First of all, the most representative is state-owned enterprises, as well as state-owned shareholding and holding enterprises, which naturally have political connections. In addition, Jia Ming and Zhang Zhe (2010) believe that enterprises can also establish political connections through their executives acting as deputies to the NPC or members of the CPPCC. Among the executives, the leaders of state-owned enterprises are often government officials with high administrative ranks. Besides, many private enterprises employ the government officials who have been retired or engaged in business deals as executives, as their related connections will remain despite the fact that they no longer have power after retirement or engagement in business. What's more, even if the executives did not or did act as officials, they are still able to participate in political affairs or deliberations of the government by means of becoming members of the CPPCC and deputies to the NPC, and even influence the decisions of the government.

However, political connection differs from government intervention and political corruption, where the main difference between political connection and government intervention lies in the subject of analysis. The analytical subject of political connections is enterprises, which establish political connections for the purpose of establishing contacts with the departments or officials of the government so as to achieve their own interests, while the analytical subject of government intervention is the government, which achieves a certain public purpose or the private interests of officials by intervening in the operation and management of enterprises (Bertr et al., 2004). In addition, political corruption mainly refers to the practice that enterprises obtain illegal benefits from the government or officials by illegal means. Although political connection enables the enterprises to enhance their competitiveness, it is mainly achieved through better understanding of policies and better communication with the government, which is usually legitimate.

To sum up, political connection is a legitimate implicit relationship constructed by an enterprise on its own initiative with the owner of political rights. To be specific, it is mainly achieved through the personal relations of executives, or the identity of members of the CPPCC, deputies to the NPC and members of the Congress.

Institutional Environment

Institutions are a number of political, social regulations, laws and regulations designed to boost production and enhance distribution efficiency, while different institutional arrangements may lead to varied market transaction costs (North & Thomas, 1973). Institutional environment acts upon the efficiency of factor allocation to affect the economic growth of the region, investigate the proportion of economic resources allocated based on market, reduce government intervention, alleviate the burden of enterprises beyond tax, and shrink the government size (Fang, 2011). As the subject of macroeconomic regulation and control, the government engaged in resource allocation plays an indisputable role in stabilizing the economy and achieving equity. However, excessive and inappropriate government intervention is also likely to exert a negative impact and reduce economic efficiency. Therefore, a benign and moderate relationship between the government and the market is essential for economic development (North, 1990). Entrepreneurs are important resources, but the pace of scientific and technological progress and productivity development in a society depends on where the limited resources of entrepreneurs are directed by the institution of the society. Baumol divides the types of entrepreneurs' activities into productive activities and unproductive activities, while different institutional environments and organizational modes determine the relative amount of remuneration that entrepreneurs of different types can obtain, which also affects the allocation of investments in productive activities and unproductive activities by entrepreneurs in the pursuit of profit maximization (Baumol, 1990). Generally speaking, the more resources the government controls and the higher the proportion of economic resources allocated is, the less freedom enterprises will have to obtain resources through the market, and the more likely it is to induce the unproductive rent-seeking behavior of entrepreneurs and enterprises (Liu & Tang, 2013).

Structure of the Book

This book is mainly divided into six parts, and the major contents and the structure can be referred to in Figure 1.1 below:

Chapter 1 is Introduction, which mainly introduces the realistic and theoretical background of this study, and then puts forward the corresponding research questions. In the meantime, combined with the research questions, it gives a brief introduction into the corresponding logical thinking and the research methods to be adopted, as well as the main concepts of the book.

Chapter 2 is Literature Review, which mainly introduces the relevant theories according to the research topic of this book, and reviews the research literature and conclusions of financial fraud based on these theories. The main purpose of this chapter is to pave the way for the theoretical building of this book through theoretical dialogue and comments.

Chapter 3 is Theoretical Analysis and Research Hypotheses, which mainly puts forward the corresponding solutions to the research questions, and gives the relationship between institutional factors, such as institutional environment and political connection, and financial fraud, based on the theoretical dialogue with existing research, and explores the specific mechanism. Finally, a model is constructed according to the theory, and the corresponding theoretical hypotheses are proposed.

Chapter 4 is Research Design, which mainly introduces the samples selected for the empirical study of this book and the measurement methods of related research concepts, and designs the corresponding test methods and models.

Chapter 5 is Hypothesis Testing and Result Analysis, which first carries out a descriptive statistical analysis of samples pursuant to the data collected, and then conducts a hypothesis test according to the hypotheses and model design, and finally discusses the results of empirical research.

Chapter 6 is Research Conclusion and Prospects, which summarizes the results based the conclusion and analysis of the research, points out the shortcomings of the research, and puts forward the research prospects in this field.

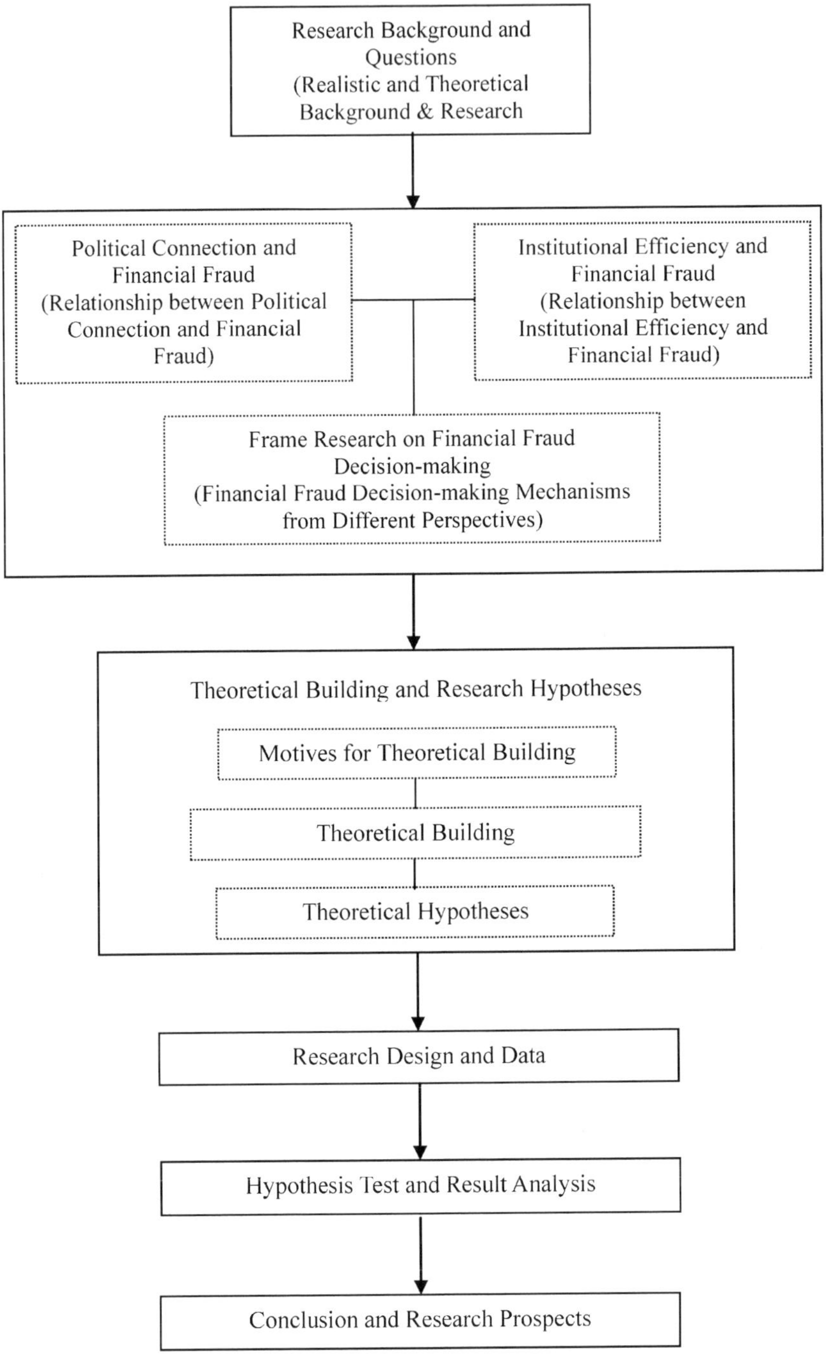

Figure 1-1 Structure of the Book

Chapter 2 Literature Review

In the decades since the issue of financial fraud was put forward, the practical problems arising from the phenomenon have become increasingly prominent and the methods have become increasingly concealed, which have seriously damaged the stability of the securities market and the individual interests of investors. In this regard, scholars at home and abroad have discussed the formation and influence mechanisms of financial fraud from different perspectives, and developed a number of representative theoretical achievements. On the basis of a comprehensive review of literatures concerning financial fraud, this chapter mainly combs and summarizes the key theoretical perspectives, such as prospect theory, institutional efficiencies and political connection, as well as the existing research on related influencing factors. In this section, the connotation of prospect theory and its influence on prospect theory are expounded.

Review of Studies on Enterprise Decision-making Based on Prospect Theory

Historical Origin of Behavioral Decision-making

Since Aristotle's time in ancient Greece, man has been regarded as a rational animal by philosophers, and man's behavior is based on rationality. Only under extreme special conditions such as fatigue, drunkenness and anger may people make irrational decisions with irrational thinking. Therefore, normal people not only have reasonable reasoning ability, but also have standardized rationality and decision-making principles, where the rational decision-making principles can be manifested in their ideas and actions. Traditional economics, based on the hypothesis of rational man and the maximization of individual interests, believes that decision makers own complete information and are able to make a comprehensive trade-off on this basis so as to achieve the optimal choice.

Rational decision theory pursues Pareto optimality based on the hypothesis of perfect rationality so as to maximize the interests of individuals. The traditional rational decision theory can be described as that the actor is rational and the information is complete, which means that the individual can get all the information related to the decision, and that under such complete information, the individual has stable preferences accordingly. For this reason, the individual actor must be able to screen all the schemes according to complete information and stable preferences, and ultimately make optimal decisions. Utility and subjective probability are the two theoretical foundations of rational decision theory. Under the hypothesis of perfect rationality, rational decision theory is not based on the actual experimental data, but directly depends on the hypothetical reasoning made by such hypothesis. In the 1950s, Savage constructed the theoretical framework of subjective expected utility theory, which enabled statistical decision theory based on rigorous philosophical basis and axiomatic framework to emerge and develop. Later, Savage, Raiffa, Howard and other scholars, on this basis, carried out a decision-making analysis by means of Bayes analysis tools, and then perfected the analysis framework of the statistical decision theory.

In the 1960s, the analytical method of statistical decision theory shifted from the original optimal statistical decision model to practical application, thereby making considerable progress and ultimately enabling the rational decision theory to gradually perfect in the 1960s and 1970s. From then on, the main research contents of decision-making theory had a close bearing on the normative decision-making theory, which regarded the hypothesis of perfect rationality as a logical starting point. Based on the scientific research law going from special to general, the decision-maker aims at maximizing his own interests and conforms to Von Neumann and Morgenstern (VNM), and conducts normative research on the decision makers by constructing a mathematical model. Therefore, rational decision theory belongs to the research field of normative economics. Moreover, rational decision theory adopts a standardized paradigm of economic research, with the aim of building an entirely rational, optimal and universal decision model. In view of this, the rational decision theory can improve the effect and efficiency of decision-making to a certain extent, but it fails to completely solve the problem of the effectiveness of decision-making behavior.

In 1947, on the premise of a rigorous hypothesis of individual rationality, Von Neumann and Morgenstem established a rational decision model, expected utility theory, by means of rigorous logical analysis and mathematical reasoning, which marked the birth of rational decision theory. After that, Savage constructed the subjective probability inference by Bayes statistical analysis in 1954, which enriched the theoretical basis of rational decision theory. Subsequently, R. A. Howard and H. Raiffa tried to apply the relevant theoretical research results to practice. At the same time, from the late 1950s, many scholars began to study rational decision theory from a psychological point of view, to examine its authenticity in practice, to study whether the actual decision-making behavior of decision makers conforms to the ideas of J. Von Neumarm & Morgen and L.J. Savage and to explore the causes of the inconsistency, all of which led to the birth of behavioral decision theory. Researchers of behavioral decision making, represented by Ward Edwards, carried out empirical studies to compare the actual decision-making behavior of the rational decision model with that of the decision makers, and found that the rational decision model is often deviated in practical application.

Any field of scientific research has its historical benchmark. In the field of decision-making and judgment, the benchmark is Ward Edwards' article "The Theory of Decision Making" published in Psychological Bulletin in 1954 (Naylor, 1994), which is because Edwards, as the pioneer of the subjective expected utility maximization model, believes that subjective probability does not necessarily follow the objective law, and that the cognitive illusion of decision makers is most likely to lead to the deviation between intuitive judgment and the expected utility value decision model. Edwards (1961) found that the subjective expected utility model works poorly in the prediction of gambling decision-making. Later, he put forward the concept of subjective probability in 1962, and argued that the sum of subjective probability may not be equal to 1. In the same year, he pointed out that weight function could be allowed to vary according to the types of expected results. Subsequently, Later, Kahneman and Tversky proposed prospect theory in 1979, based on the special case of the model proposed by Edwards in 1962.

The idea of weight has a significant and far-reaching impact on the studies of psychologists represented by Kahneman and Tversky. Therefore, Edwards not only studied the subjective expected utility model, but also laid the foundation for the early research on Bayes inference. In view of the contradiction between rational decision model and the actual decision-making behavior of the decision makers, one branch of decision-making theory research tries to continuously improve and revise the existing expected utility theory along the track of rational decision-making, while the other branch attempts to open up the trajectory of behavioral decision-making, and to analyze and explore the mechanism of the actual decision-making behavior of the decision makers. Slovic (1972), as a researcher exploring the process of investment decision-making based on the results of psychological research, believes that it is more helpful for decision makers to recognize the limitations of human beings than to hold that mankind is infallible. Simon put forward a method of information processing and decision-making based on bounded rationality in 1997. These research results, coupled with Tversky's heuristic selection rules centered on the elimination rule of aspects and Kahneman's and Tversky's expectation theory, constitute the most representative theoretical research results in the field of behavioral decision theory. The core of all these models is to describe how the decision makers make decisions from all feasible alternatives, and try to apply these theories to practice. The theory is applied in the field of finance as behavioral finance.

In particular, it is worth mentioning that, Herbert Simon (1978), Maurice Allais (1988) and Daniel Kahneman (2002), three researchers in the field of behavioral decision-making, won the Nobel Prize in Economic Sciences, which is because that economics is, in the final analysis, a study of human choice. In light of this, it is more important to study the behavioral decision theory from the perspectives of how people think, how they solve the problems, how they make decisions and how they can improve their ability to solve problems and formulate policies.

Xi Kaiyuan (2004), the latest representative in the field of behavioral decision-making, pointed out that "Human perception is often highly selective, memory is full of deviations, and the results of different schemes are often misunderstood. Therefore, there is no decision that does not depend on the situation, while the decisions and judgments people make depend on the way they view and interpret the world, which are all affected by selective perception, the pressure of maintaining cognitive consistency, memory deviation and situation changes." Xi's contribution to behavioral decision theory lies in his proposition of hedonomics aiming at maximizing people's happiness in a broad sense. Based on the above-mentioned behavior theories summarized and arranged, the development stages of behavioral decision theory can be roughly divided into three stages of germination stage, growth stage and maturity stage.

The first stage was the germination stage of behavioral decision theory, lasting from the 1950s to the mid-1970s, during which the research achievements were dominated by the achievements made in the research on the defects of rational decision theory. It belonged to the antecedent stage of normative research, and thus failed to become a new research field. The research methods were mainly psychological experimental methods to find out the psychological reasons that influence the decision makers to judge and make a choice by means of psychological experiments. Then, the influence mechanism of these psychological reasons on judgment and choice was explored, so as to achieve the goal of describing and interpreting the decision makers' specific decision-making process of judgment and choice. In a word, the study of decision-making behavior in this period was still at a shallow level, while the behavioral decision theory did not attract enough attention from the academic circles.

The second stage was the growth stage, lasting from the mid-1970s to the mid-late 1980s, during which behavioral decision theory had become an independent discipline and was widely used in the fields of economy, finance and management. At this time, the research object of behavioral decision-making was extended to all aspects of the decision-making process of the decision makers, and the research methods involved a variety of methods, such as observation, investigation and experimental methods, and some models that described behavioral decision-making based on actual decision-making behavior were constructed. The representative theory during this period was the prospect theory by Kahaeman and Tversky, which not only used psychology to improve and revise the basic hypotheses of traditional economics, but also summed up the decisions that deviate from the traditional optimal behavior after a large number of economic and psychological experiments. Then the complexity and uncertainty of the decision makers' decision-making behavior were proposed, and the deterministic effect, isolation effect and reflection effect of the decision makers in risk decision-making were ultimately explained very well. On this basis, the prospect theory at this time was called the first-generation prospect theory by later scholars.

The third stage was the maturity stage, lasting from the mid-late 1980s to the present, during which the major achievements were to summarize behavioral characteristics, refine behavioral variables and summarize them into the research framework of rational decision-making. At this time, scholars constantly revised and replaced the decision model, and studied the role of the cognitive limitations, subjective psychological factors of the decision and the environment on the decision-making psychology of the decision makers, as well as the impact of alternatives and environment on decision-making, which not only improves the general applicability of the decision model, but also promotes the behavioral decision theory to ultimately become mature. It is particularly worth mentioning that the research contents in the financial field, represented by the behavioral asset pricing model, the behavioral portfolio model, the BSV model (Barberis-Shleffer-Vishny Model), the DHS model (Daniel-Hirsheifer-Subramanyam Model), the HS model (Hong-Stein Model) and the BHS model (Barberis-Huang-Santos Model) and other investor mentality models, occupied a leading position during this period.

At the same time, the first-generation prospect theory has developed to the second and third generations with the unremitting efforts of scholars. Based on the exploration into probabilistic transformation, the second-generation prospect theory is developed into a cumulative prospect theory based on hierarchical decision weight, which not only investigates the prospects of uncertainty and risk, but also analyzes the loss and benefit. Therefore, it has been extensively used in the fields of theoretical research and practical application due to its ability to explain the decision makers' structural effects, non-linearity of preferences, resource dependence, risk pursuit and loss avoidance during the selection experiment in a perfect manner. Fundamentally speaking, the first and second generations of prospect theory, because of the limitations of fixed reference points for prospects, are unable to be applied to practical behavioral decision-making problems such as gambling and opportunity trading, such as stock trading and insurance. Based on this, Ulrich

Schmidti et al. proposed the third-generation prospect theory (PT3) in 2005 on the basis of further explanation of preference reversal, which developed the fixed reference points to uncertain points on the basis of inheriting the previous prospect theories. In this way, it not only expands the research content of prospect theory, but also enables the preference reversal of the decision makers in practical behavior to be predicted.

Rationality has been given different meanings in different fields. In the field of philosophy, rationality is regarded as the cognitive ability of human beings. In the field of psychology, rationality is regarded as a cognitive, inferential or problem-solving process. In the field of sociology, rationality is considered as the conscious adaptability of organizational goals. In the field of economics, rationality is considered an attribute of the action plan selected during the selection process. As a result, it can be seen that the meaning of rationality has been criticized, revised and developed by researchers of different disciplines with the continuous development of behavioral science. With this constant questioning and criticism of rational thought, many researchers began to pay attention to the research of imperfect rationality, that is, bounded rationality.

Modern Decision-making Theory and Questions about Perfect Rationality

Modern decision-making theory stems from questioning rational decision-making. Neither the expected utility theory by Von Neumann and Morgenstem nor Savage's subjective expected utility theory fully considers the psychological factors of the decision makers, while they merely conduct quantitative analysis under the premise of rational hypotheses. Therefore, they have lost the ability to explain many behaviors in the actual analysis of economic life due to their extremely simple and ideal hypotheses. In 1948, Preston and Barattai compared the row selection model of Von Neumann and Morgenstem's expected utility theory with the experimental results and raised corresponding doubts. In 1953, French economist Maurice Allais put forward the famous Allais Paradox, pointing out that the behavior of the actor is contrary to the analysis results of the expected utility theory. In 1961, Daniel Ellsberg put forward the Ellsberg Paradox, pointing out that, in the real economic life, actors usually make decisions based on their subjective probability, rather than the so-called objective probability distribution.

From 1982 to 1986, Kahneman and Tversky carried out a number of behavioral experiments in the laboratory, and the results showed that the decision-making choices of the actors may vary even if they are faced with the same decision-making question expressed in different ways. With the continuous questioning of rational decision theory, many researchers began to think about the behavioral hypothesis of the actor, while the people were aware of the fact that the actor was irrational. In 1978, Herbert A. Simon won the Nobel Prize in Economic Sciences. Taking this as an opportunity, bounded rationality theory was widely recognized. Moreover, Simon's decision-making theory based on bounded rationality is also regarded as the beginning of modern decision-making theory, while modern decision-making theory adopts a descriptive paradigm for research based on practical experience, with an aim of seeking the law of decision-making behavior on the basis of human substantive behavior with the aid of the research contents of behavioral science and psychology.

Modern decision-making theory can be divided into two research areas according to the different perspectives and analysis methods for bounded rationality. One is to perfect the rational decision-making model by means of operational research and cybernetics and other methods and theories, as well as to introduce fuzzy mathematics in order to increase the uncertain premise of decision-making problems, while the other is to introduce the relevant contents of psychology, sociology and logic to explore the psychological changes of the decision makers and their changing mechanism in the process of decision-making, as well as the behavior of these individuals and social factors, and to lay stress on the describing the personality characteristics and emotional cognition of the actors, in order to find out how these factors affect the decision-making process of the actors.

Bounded Rationality

Kenneth J. Arrow (1951) first proposed the concept of bounded rationality, believing that human behavior has conscious rationality, but the rationality is bounded. Douglass C.North believed that “Human finitude has two meanings. First, the environment is complex, and people are faced with a complex and uncertain world in the form of impersonal exchange. The more transactions there are, the more uncertain it will be and the less complete the information will be. Second, people have bounded ability to calculate and know the environment, as it is possible to know everything." Herbert Simon (1947) pointed out the unrealities of neoclassical economics, put forward the thinking of bounded rationality and pioneered a new field of decision-making behavior theory. Furthermore, he believes that it is impossible for individuals to obtain the complete information needed to make rational decisions in a complex society, which determines the bounded rationality of human beings. In this regard, there is no way for people to make perfectly rational decisions after taking into account all the problems. In practical social life, people tend to make decisions based on their previous experience, which is a heuristic method.

The research of bounded rationality can be divided into the following three stages according to the development process of the thought and theory of bounded rationality:

First, it is the germination stage. At this time, bounded rationality was mainly regarded as an idea, while scholars studied the internal causes of bounded rationality mainly by means of qualitative description. For instance, Simon (1983) attributed bounded rationality to the lack of cognitive ability for individuals. Rubinstein (1986) argues that the lack of propensity and cognitive ability leads to bounded rationality. Conlisk (1996) argues that bounded rationality stems from the complex cost and incentive mechanisms in the decision-making process of decision makers. Behavior decision-making scientists, represented by Kahneman and Tversky, attribute bounded rationality to exceptions in the process of decision-making. Furthermore, Kahneman & Tversky (1984), Thaler (1985), Arkes & Blumer (1985) and Pulford & Colman (1996) attributed bounded rationality to framing effect, mental accounting, sunk cost fallacys and overconfidence, respectively. On the basis of defining the concept of bounded rationality, domestic scholars have studied its characteristics and explored its psychological roots from the perspective of psychology.

Second, it is a period of theoretical exploration and development. Scholars have constructed several bounded rationality models based on a large number of standardized studies and discussions. Luce (1959) established the Logit model, which integrates the coefficient of bounded rationality into the selection probability skillfully, thus becoming the initial model of bounded rationality. Based on Luce's Logit model, Shesheinski (2003) explores bounded rationality of individuals with the social welfare function. Since then, a number of scholars both at home and abroad, including Basov (2005), Rubinstein et al. (1997), Saari Donald (1995), Francesca Beccacece and Lesandra Cillo (2006), have described the phenomenon and behavior of bounded rationality from different angles, such as cost effect, static and dynamic laws and procedural characteristics, and proposed their respective models, including inframarginal analysis, static model, dynamic model of Markov Chain, descriptive bounded rational model, geometric descriptive model, target-based benchmark program model and so forth. In view of the complexity of the causes of bounded rationality, only a small number of achievements have been made in the research on the modeling of the internal mechanism of bounded rationality, among which the representative models include Kahneman's prospect theory, Tversky's exclusion theory and Stirling’s internal rational model. At the same time, many domestic scholars have also explored and studied the internal mechanism of bounded rationality by means of simulation methods, such as evolutionary game model, for interactive rationality and group rationality. However, due to the fact that these studies on the internal mechanism are still unable to get rid of the scope of research of perfect rationality hypothesis, there are some limitations in the related research. Moreover, scholars have thoroughly studied and developed their understanding of bounded rationality, which has led to the unprecedented development of axiomatic basis research. In addition, many researchers have constructed some bounded rationality models by modifying or weakening the rational conditions in traditional theory. For instance, Baigent and Gaertner (1996) modified the optimization criterion to the politeness decision rule. Besides, some other scholars have constructed a new bounded rationality model based on the theoretical and experimental results of behavioral science and psychology.

Third, it is the application stage. Despite the fact that the scholars have not made satisfactory achievements in the theoretical research on the causes and modeling of bounded rationality, some of them have still devoted themselves to applying the ideas and theories of bounded rationality to the studies in economics and management. As a result, the major contributions in this stage lie in the applications of the concept and model of bounded rationality, including the research on asset pricing, behavioral finance, social organizational structure, market management and transportation scheduling. There are some defects in the current concept and model of bounded rationality, but the bounded rationality model, in these specific application areas, has the ability to explain and describe actual decision-making and management problems that perfect rationality can not.

Prospect Theory

Kahneman & Tversky (1979) published an article entitled Prospect Theory: An Analysis of Decision under Risk in Econometrica, which conducted a systematic summary and analysis of the heuristic strategies such as representativeness, availability, anchoring & adjustment, framing effect and their cognitive effects, which are ubiquitous in the process of risk decision-making, and then proposes prospect theory on the basis of a number of psychological experiments, which can better explain the phenomenon that people are systematically divorced from the circumstances predicted by the expected utility theory in real life.

The main viewpoints of prospect theory are as follows:

Reference dependence: When making a decision, people tend to set a reference point in advance, and weigh the income or loss according to the point, and thus they are more impressed by the change of wealth rather than the final amount.

Risk reference reversal: In the vicinity of the reference point, people's risk preference will be reversed, while people tend to hold a risk-averse attitude towards income and a risk-seeking attitude towards loss;

Loss aversion: Faced with the same amount of income and loss, people's aversion of loss is greater than their preference to income;

Diminishing sensitivity: The farther away it is from the reference point, the smaller the impact of the marginal changes in income or loss on people's mentality will be, which is similar to the law of diminishing marginal utility;

Non-linear decision weight: When making decisions, people will transform the original probability of an event into a non-linear decision weight, and often overestimate the small probability events and underestimate the large probability events.

Prospect theory is the core theory to investigate the logic of enterprises' strategic decisions (Kahneman & Tversky, 2013), which lays a foundation for the analysis of the adjustment of enterprises' strategic decisions. March & Simon (1958) believe that the expected level is a weighted function of past goals, past performance of the organization, and the past performance of other organizations. The decision makers of bounded rationality tend to decide the follow-up behavior decisions based on the gap between the actual performance and the expected level. In case that the actual performance is lower than the expected level, the decision maker will define such state below expectation as a state of loss. When the actual performance is higher than the expected level, the decision maker will define the state above expectation as a state of gain. Based on different business conditions, decision makers will make completely different decisions. When the performance of an enterprise fails to reach the expected level, it will trigger the problem-seeking behavior of the enterprise, and ultimately lead to strategic change. When the performance of an enterprise reaches the expected level, the enterprise tends to maintain the status quo and avoid those behaviors that are likely to lead to a decline in performance (Bromiley et al., 2001).

Prospect theory revises the cost-benefit analysis mechanism of traditional economics from the perspective of relative utility, which is because people usually make decisions based on the gap between reality and expectation in the real situations, rather than the absolute cost-benefit analysis. However, the expectation gradually comes into being in the process of long-term and repeated decision-making and performance evaluation. Expectations based on past experience, in turn, affect the future strategic choice of the organization (Cyert & March, 1963; Greve, 1998; Greve, 2003; Greve, 2003). The decision model based on performance feedback (Greve, 2003) has laid the keynote of the current research on enterprises' strategic decisions and provided an effective theoretical basis for the analysis of enterprise strategic choice at the practical level.

Today, more than 30 years after its publication, prospect theory is still the best choice to interpret the risk decision-making behavior of human beings in an experimental environment, and the two founders won the 2002 Nobel Prize (Barberis, 2013). In recent years, behavioral economists have made a lot of useful supplements to the prospect theory, making it increasingly consistent with economics. Their efforts have yielded remarkable results, as not only has the theoretical system of prospect theory become more and more abundant and practical, but also there have been many empirical studies to test the relevant theories. Specifically speaking, the current studies on prospect theory can be divided into the following categories:

Theoretical Studies on the Criticism and Contrast of Prospect Theory

These studies mainly focus on the comparison between prospect theory and related competitive theory, among which the most prominent is the comparative study between prospect theory and expected utility theory. Expected utility theory is an economic decision-making theory based on the hypothesis of optimization, while prospect theory is a decision-making theory based on the hypothesis of the satisfaction principle, which is closer to the actual decision-making situation. However, in reality, people seldom act according to the optimal prediction results, but it does not mean that the expected utility theory is of no value in the process of actual decision-making. The expected utility theory and prospect theory are neither superior nor inferior to each other, but they are just strategic choices under different situations. On the one hand, the expected utility theory is a normative theory derived from a number of axiomatic hypotheses through rigorous logical reasoning and mathematical deduction. On the other hand, prospect theory is a descriptive theory based on a series of psychological experiments. The relevant parameters in the model should be estimated by statistics based on survey and experimental data. In summary, the expected utility theory and prospect theory are based on different theoretical hypotheses and research paradigms, so that they naturally have varied scopes of application. Van de Kaa (2010) found that when people have more decision-making information in hand and are more familiar with decision-making environment and results, the predicted results of expected utility theory are more consistent with people's actual choices, and that when people have insufficient decision-making information and less understanding of decision-making environment and results, it is better to make decisions based on the prospect theory.

As prospect theory is a less mature theory, it has aroused a great many doubts from some economists since it was proposed, which are mainly reflected in the following aspects:

First, the decision weight function is defined based on objective probability, but the objective probability of events in real life can seldom be foreseen;

Second, the parameter values in prospect theory are usually not fixed, but influenced by specific decision-making situations and vary from person to person, which makes it difficult to be applied to practice;

Third, the formation of reference points involves a very complex psychological process. At present, people have no idea about how the reference points are formed and what affect the points, while the selection of reference points is strongly related to the subjective preferences of researchers;

Fourth, as a static decision-making theory, prospect theory can not describe the dynamic process of human beings making decisions by learning and adjustment to adapt to the changes;

Fifth, because of the external validity of the experiment, the prospect theory based on psychological experiments may not have universal explanatory power.

In order to enhance the ability of prospect theory to interpret and predict reality, some researchers have expanded it on the basis of inheriting the basic hypotheses of prospect theory. Thus, in order to better explain the preference reversal phenomenon, Schmidt et al. (2008) introduced the concept of dynamic reference point based on the original prospect theory and proposed the concept of the third-generation prospect theory. In addition, Van de Kaa (2010) proposed the concept of extended prospect theory so as to apply prospect theory to empirical research and consider the heterogeneity of the actor.

Camerer (2004) pointed out that the expected utility theory, prospect theory, and other relevant theories which draw on or integrate some factors of these two theories fail to completely describe the characteristics of human beings in the process of general decision-making, and to give a clear explanation of optimization for the existing data. Ross & Ward (1995) also believe that there is no theory that can replace the expected utility theory, which constitutes part of the abstract economic model as a general human decision model. Moreover, prospect theory and other alternative theories are quite effective solutions to some special issues, but they can not replace the expected utility theory. Van Wee (2010) pointed out that Van Wee (2010) pointed out that researchers should not confine themselves to a particular theory until they reach a specific conclusion, but should analyze the psychological motivation and behavioral characteristics of the testees or respondents in depth according to the research hypothesis and the data they can collect, and balance different theories. Therefore, prospect theory and other theories other than the expected utility theory should not be regarded as alternative theories of expected utility theory. In case that all kinds of theories are merely part of truth, all theories should be able to learn from and integrate with each other to form a complete theoretical picture, which reflects the unity of science. What's more, different theories should complement each other, absorb and draw lessons from each other, and even integrate with each other. Only in this way can the gap between theoretical prediction and actual results be narrowed continuously. In fact, throughout all the studies of economic behavior, there are still many behavioral theories besides expected utility theory and prospect theory, which are also developed on the basis of questioning and challenging the expected utility theory, and have made considerable achievements in their respective scopes of application.

Studies on Optimization and Expansion of Prospect Theory

As mentioned above, one of the important reasons why prospect theory is not applied in all aspects of economics is that there are some difficulties in its application. A core idea of prospect theory is that people's utility stems from the comparison of gain or loss on the basis of a specific reference. However, in any case, the definition of gain or loss is ambiguous, because Kahneman & Tversky (1979) did not provide too many criteria for the reference frame setting when putting forward the theory.

From a strategic point of view, assuming that we need to predict a listed company's preferences for positive and negative risk-taking behaviors with the prospect theory, we should first set the definition of gain or loss for this company. Do they measure gain or loss from the perspective of overall benefits or loss avoidance? Are they concerned about long-term returns or short-term stability? Even if we can confirm that the company measures gain or loss from the perspective of long-term returns, is it only when the market value of the company is positive that can it be identified as a state of gain? Or is it gain only when the market value exceeds the value at some point in the past, or is it only when the expected return of the investor has to be achieved? Further, do investors measure gain or loss in yearly units, or in monthly units, or do they focus only on weekly fluctuations (Kőszegi & Rabin, 2007; 2009) ? In their research, the two scholars provided an analytical framework compatible with various situations for the application of prospect theory in economics, which is to measure gain or loss by taking expectation as a reference. To be concrete, utility is understood as the gap between actual consumption experience and expected consumption experience. Thus, utility model also conforms to the principle of loss avoidance and diminishing marginal utility. Furthermore, in order to make the frame more practical, they assume that expectations are rational, which has greatly increased the probability that prospect theory will be used in subsequent studies, especially in the fields other than finance.

According to the theory of behavioral corporate finance, different decision makers obviously vary from each other in terms of the level of psychological cognition and background characteristics. Whether it is the irrational behavior decision-making of the decision maker arising from the cognitive psychological preference or the difference of the preference and decision-making of the decision-maker's individual characteristics and life experience, it means that the internal factors of the individual decision makers have played a certain role. MacCrimmon and Wehrung (1986) analyzed and studied the personal characteristics of 509 senior managers from the United States and Canada, which are closely related to risk, and then drew a conclusion that the older managers with more seniority are inclined to risk aversion, while those with higher education, higher positions and power in smaller enterprises are inclined to risk preference.

Then MacCrimmon and Wehrung (1990) summarized the characteristics that led to decision makers' risk preference into three aspects:

Firstly, personal traits, including age, independence, educational level and nationality of decision makers;

Secondly, economic conditions, including wealth and income;

Thirdly, occupational characteristics, including position, power, seniority, company size and industry, etc.

Moreover, they are classified into the following categories by means of factor analysis:

Firstly, power, income, wealth and position, closely related to success;

Secondly, age, seniority and independence, closely related to maturity;

Thirdly, nationality and education, closely related to Canadian-low education;

Fourthly, the scale of industry and company, closely related to big banks.

Through empirical research, they found that the more successful senior managers are more inclined to risk preference, while the more mature senior managers and those from big banks are more inclined to risk aversion. In addition, a great many senior managers believe that their risk preferences are stable. For instance, successful senior managers hold that they have a stronger risk preference than other senior managers, while mature senior managers hold that they have a lower risk preference than other senior managers, which can be reflected by the difference between the senior managers in terms of personal debt and gambling behavior.

Williams and Narendran (1999) studied the determinants of decision-makers' risk decision-making behavior, and summarized the personal characteristics of decision-makers which affected their risk preferences and ultimately led to the differentiation of risk decision-making behavior into four aspects, namely, demographic factors, work-related factors, organization-related factors and personal characteristics, among which the demographic factors mainly refer to age, gender, education, culture and nationality, work-related factors mainly refer to tenure, working hours and power levels, organization-related factors mainly refer to industry, whether controlled by the government, organization size and organization's attitude to risk, and personal characteristics mainly refer to desire for success, internal control and tolerance of ambiguity. They conducted an empirical test on the 285 senior Indian managers living in India and Singapore, and the results showed that the male senior managers with comparatively modern cultural values who live in India have relatively high risk preference level. In addition, according to the latest theoretical research results, major events and experiences in life will exert an extensive, lasting and far-reaching impact on individual risk preference and decision-making, while the individual differences in life experience will lead to differences in the CEO's risk preference.

Elder, Gimbel and Ivie (1991) believe that war is a game between adventurers, and that the skills derived from combat enable individuals to become more confident and more capable of coping with high pressures and risks, and ultimately develop higher risk preferences and more assertive and self-confident personality characteristics for the individuals. Similarly, the empirical research by Malmendier, Tate and Yan (2010) reflected that the entrepreneurs who have undergone the wars, especially the World War II, prefer to take risks and are more tolerant of risks, which will eventually have a long-term impact on their risk preferences and risk decision-making. The empirical research of Malmendier and Nagel (2011) showed that the entrepreneurs who have undergone the Great Depression are relatively stable and invest much less in risk assets, which is because the experience of the economic crisis has tempered the entrepreneurs' risk-taking spirit, reduced their risk tolerance and eventually they gave up the corporate investment decisions with higher risk.

Impact of Prospect Theory on Corporate Decision-making Research

In recent years, with the development of behavioral economics, the analysis of agent's behavior in enterprise decision-making research has also put forward fundamental hypotheses that are more in line with the actual situation (Pepper & Gore, 2015). Specifically, it is to introduce prospect theory into the study of agent theory to analyze agent's decision-making behavior. It should be pointed out here that, compared with the traditional principal-agent theory which triggers the discussion of the rationality of managers' decision-making from the rational perspective of managers, one of the basic premises of this study from the perspective of prospect theory is to emphasize the irrationality of managers' decision-making, which runs through all the analysis processes in the following text.

Prospect theory mainly studies the impact of expectation on enterprise decision-making. March & Simon (1958) believe that the expected level is a weighted function of past goals, past performance of the organization, and the past performance of other organizations. The decision makers of bounded rationality tend to decide the follow-up behavior decisions based on the gap between the actual performance and the expected level. In case that the actual performance is lower than the expected level, the decision maker will define such state below expectation as a state of loss. When the actual performance is higher than the expected level, the decision maker will define the state above expectation as a state of gain. Based on different comparison results, decision makers will make entirely different decisions. When the performance of an enterprise fails to reach the expected level, it will trigger the problem-seeking behavior of the enterprise, and ultimately lead to strategic change. When the performance of an enterprise reaches the expected level, the enterprise tends to maintain the status quo and avoid those behaviors that are likely to lead to a decline in performance (Bromiley et al., 2001).

With the continuous development of the securities market, enterprises have become increasingly dependent on external financing and the expectations of external stakeholders on corporate performance are increasingly influencing the decision-making of enterprises. These stakeholders are mainly divided into three categories. The first type of external governance mechanism is the owners of enterprises (Brav et al., 2008; Hoskisson et al., 2009). Researchers mainly focus on institutional investors, such as mutual funds, hedge funds, pension funds, banks, insurance companies and donations, to verify the impact of shareholders on corporate output (Goranova et al., 2010). Specialized institutional investors raise higher requirements for supervision and control capabilities. Porter (1992) describes special owners as those who hold a large proportion of the small number of corporate stocks for a long time, who are strongly motivated to supervise and manage, and are able to grasp and understand a large amount of complex information about the companies they invest in. The second type of external governance is managers. In consideration of the future career development, their business performance is also widely concerned by the professional managers market. Such pressure from external evaluation will prompt managers to continuously optimize corporate governance. The third category is rating agencies, such as securities analysis, or external analysts. With the development of securities market, more and more attention has been paid to this form of governance, and a growing number of companies are constantly adjusting their strategies in order to meet the expectations of analysts and thus leave a better impression in the minds of investors (Chen et al., 2015; Wiersema & Zhang, 2011). In addition to these three dimensions, there are other external forces that will also have an impact on enterprises, such as the legal system and social action, but we still confine our research to these three points, because they are the most important and influential form of external governance of agent's behavior.

There are two different viewpoints on the relationship between stakeholder expectations and corporate decision-making in existing studies:

One is from the perspective of positive promotion. Relevant scholars believe that the expectations of stakeholders can effectively motivate the motivations of agents to make achievements and prompt them to work hard to improve their bargaining power in the manager market and enhance the performance of enterprises. However, the expectation gradually comes into being in the process of long-term and repeated decision-making and performance evaluation. Expectations based on past experience, in turn, affect the future strategic choice of the organization (Cyert & March, 1963; Greve, 1998; Greve, 2003; Greve, 2003). It is one of the new changes that prospect theory brings to the study of enterprise decision-making to discuss the agent's specific strategic decision-making in order to meet the expectations of stakeholders. Moreover, the decision model based on performance feedback lays the keynote of the frontier research of enterprise decision-making, and also provides an effective theoretical basis for the analysis of enterprise strategic choice at the practical level (Greve, 2003).

The other is from the perspective of negative weakening. Some scholars believe that excessive external rewards or punishments may subvert a person's intrinsic motivation for moral behavior (Bertelli, 2006; Georgellis et al., 2011). That is to say, people are born with the need to autonomously control and be competent for a task (Ryan & Deci, 2000). The autonomy is concerned about the perception of choice, self-will and self-determination, while competence focuses on the belief that can exert a significant impact on the outcome (Stone et al., 2009). The autonomy and competence perceived by a person have an important impact on his internal drive (Deci & Ryan, 2012; Gagne & Deci, 2005). When external expectations conflict with individual perceptions of autonomy, it will reduce the motivation of individuals to act in the desired direction of external control (Osterloh et al., 2002). Based on this idea, a number of management studies support the view that external influences reduce the motivation of individuals to keep pace with their responsibilities for enterprises (Jacquart & Armstrong, 2013; Barkema, 1995). Osterloh & Frey (2000) found that high external stimulus will reduce employees' intrinsic motivation to organize the citizens, thereby reducing the sharing of tacit knowledge. In the same way, Sundaramurthy & Lewis (2003) argue that senior managers will lower their desire to work hard if they frequently perceive the depression from external control.

Therefore, external stakeholders tend to reduce the possibility of managers violating corporate rules by enhancing their supervision and control (Davidoff, 2013). Standard schools of economics, including agent theory, measure the need for external driving forces to prevent managers from engaging in fraud within the framework of the relative costs and benefits that may arise from the fraud (Becker, 1976). Under these theoretical frameworks, a large number of empirical studies have found that external governance mechanisms based on supervision and self-discipline are effective solutions to reduce the probability of enterprises engaging in violations (Beasley et al., 2000; Chen et al., 2006). According to the theory of cognitive development, managers will take into account the balance between internal and external motivations in the process of continuous decision-making (Boivie et al., 2012; Pepper & Gore, 2015), among which the internal motivation refers to the motivation that managers intend to complete their own job on their own initiative so as to achieve their own values and the external motivation comes from the expectations and supervision pressure of the board of directors and shareholders. We further use the cognitive evaluation theory (Deci & Ryan, 1985) and argue that the external governance mechanism will bring the high external expectations to managers as an external driving force, which will squeeze out the internal driving force of managers themselves and reduce their willingness to complete their own job of their own will. For this reason, the external governance mechanism is also likely to have an adverse effect on preventing the enterprises from violations from the perspective of the overall effect.

To sum up, there are different views on the relationship between external governance mechanism and enterprises engaging in violations in academic circles. The positive view is that external expectation is beneficial to enhance the agent's achievement motivation, thereby reducing the possibility of enterprises engaging in violations, while the negative view is that external governance will reduce the actor's management autonomy and promote the rationalization process of his or her violation, thus increasing the possibility of enterprises engaging in violations. This book holds that the main problem that causes this logical contradiction is that there are certain regulatory factors between external governance and corporate violations, which will be further analyzed in this book.

Review of Financial Fraud Theory

There has been an extremely abundant foundation for the research of financial fraud after years of development. This section reviews the theoretical development of financial fraud and its internal logic in accordance with the sequence of historical evolution.

Research on Financial Fraud from the Perspective of Criminology

Financial fraud originated from the study of asset embezzlement from the perspective of criminology (Cressey, 1950), and then three conditions of white-collar crimes were proposed, including financial problems that can not be disclosed, opportunities for trust-based fraud and the criminal's psychological adjustment ability. These three conditions then evolved into the three elements of the fraud triangle theory under the continuous deliberation and expansion of the relevant scholars, including perceived pressure, perceived opportunity and rationalization. First of all, perceived pressure refers to the pressure from the financial problems that can not be disclosed stop decision makers from continuing to operate according to well-known routines and generates a strong motivation to get rid of existing bad conditions under the situation of financial fraud. Second, perceived opportunity refers to an opportunity arising from the fact that some loopholes in corporate governance lead to the low possibility that a fraud is discovered and disclosed. Finally, rationalization means that criminal acts tend to make the actors feel some conflicts in mind, and then if they want to continue to cover up the discomfort caused by such conflicts, they have no choice but to comfort themselves with the rationalization strategy, so that they will feel that their behavior can be understood and accepted by the public and that it is within the scope of moral tolerance.

Since the proposal of the fraud triangle theory, many scholars have expanded its scope and conducted further exploration into the characteristics of the fraudster from various perspectives under the guidance of the theory (Hermanson et al., 2006).

First of all, from the perspective of perceived pressure, Apostolou et al. (2016) analyzed tax evasion behavior and discussed the pressure elements in the fraud triangle theory in depth. They believe that, in addition to the concerns in traditional studies that the subjective pressure can make people be motivated to engage in fraud, the objective pressure generated by the higher authorities is also likely to contribute to the fraudulent practices among the subordinates. Under the pressure of the higher authorities, the fraudster itself has no subjective motive to implement fraud, but has to be involved in fraud activities because of the instructions of the higher authorities. There are essential differences between the prevention of fraud in this case and that caused by subjective motives.

Second, from the perspective of perceived opportunity, Dorminey et al. (2012) believes that from the perspective of fraudulent opportunities, the occurrence of fraudulent acts depends on the two abilities of the fraudsters. On the one hand, they need to have the ability to identify the loopholes in governance and cover up their own fraud. On the other hand, they also need to be equipped mentally to cope with the risk of being exposed and punished at any time.

Finally, from the perspective of rationalization, Albrecht et al. (2004) combines agent theory and stewardship theory to introduce the fraud triangle theory into the analysis of corporate financial fraud. Moreover, they pointed out that pressure, opportunity and rationalization are the necessary conditions for financial fraud, none of which can be dispensed with. In the meantime, they further believe that the stronger dignity and belief the managers have, the higher the pursuit of internal work satisfaction will be. That is to say, the stronger the sense of ownership is, the more difficult it is to rationalize financial fraud, and thus the less likely it is to engage in financial fraud, and vice versa. In addition, Brooks et al. (2005) also found that there is a very special type of fraudsters known as absolute fraudsters, who are unable to resist the temptation to commit fraud as long as they find an opportunity for fraud, whether they are faced with financial pressure or rationalization dilemma. Relatively speaking, the accidental fraudsters are more common, who will not take fraudulent acts until the three conditions of the fraud triangle are met simultaneously. In view of this, the fraud triangle theory can not explain the behavior of the fraudster with the characteristics of the absolute fraudster. On this basis, Beasley & Hermanson (2006) further found that there are no congenital differences between the absolute fraudster and the accidental fraudster, but they can be transformed into each other. As long as the behavior of the accidental fraudster is not discovered or exposed for a long time, it is likely that this behavior will continue and recur. In other words, in case that the fraudsters have strong anti-reconnaissance capability or the external governance and supervision are less effective, it is far more likely that the accidental fraudster will gradually rationalize its own behavior, thus transforming into an absolute fraudster.

In addition to digging deeply into the influencing factors of fraud based on the prototype of fraud triangle theory, a number of scholars have also devoted themselves to expanding the fraud triangle theory to make it closer to the real situation, among which the widely known theories include the iceberg theory, the GONE theory, the theory of fraud risk factors and the CRIME model (Kong & Yu, 2015).

According to the iceberg theory, the emergence of financial fraud is not only related to the soundness and tightness of the internal governance systems of an enterprise, but also to the financial pressure the company bears. It distinguishes the objective conditions and subjective motives of fraud and emphasizes that, besides institutional design, judging and exploring the weaknesses of human nature is also of great value to the governance of fraudulent acts (Tunley, 2011).

Holding that the fraud triangle theory had some deficiencies in the dimension of human nature, Bologna (1993) proposed the G-O-N-E theory involving four factors, greed, opportunity, need and exposure pursuant to the iceberg theory, which depicts more dimensions of human nature than the triangle theory. But the two theories have similar connotations in essence. Subsequently, Pryor et al. (1996) proposed the theory of fraud risk factors on this basis, dividing the risks that are likely to arise in the fraudulent acts into special risk factors and common risk factors, among which common risk factors are mainly related to corporate governance, such as institution and supervision, while special risk factors are related to individual factors, such as personal pursuit, moral level and so forth. Generally speaking, Bologna et al. devoted themselves to the integration of the fraud triangle theory and the iceberg theory, but they did not go beyond the scope of these two theories on the whole.

Zabihollah Rezaee (2002) proposed the CRIME model, arguing that the occurrence of financial fraud was the result of five factors, namely, cooks, recipes, incentives, monitoring and end results. Firstly, the identity and characteristics of cooks have an important impact on the occurrence of financial fraud. Especially, the identity of senior managers and their related abilities and contacts can greatly reduce the difficulty of cooks engaged in fraud. Secondly, corresponding means are needed to commit fraudulent acts and avoid supervision, among which earnings management and misleading investors by distorting facts are more common. Thirdly, in addition to the economic pressures detailed in the triangle theory as one of the incentives of financial fraud, he also believes that the self-interest, ideology and psychopathy are incentives of financial fraud, which effectively incorporates the situation of the absolute fraudster into the analytical framework. Finally, he believes that monitoring mechanism can also be divided into internal and external mechanisms. Internal monitoring comes from departments directly responsible for financial performance, such as board of directors, board of supervisors and so on, while the external monitoring comes mainly from the boards of auditors, auditors, regulators and external stakeholders, such as analysts, investors and creditors.

The above models are basically the in-depth excavation or extension of the crime motive theory, which show no essential difference in the content expounded in spite of their own characteristics, perspectives and dimensions. The research of crime agent mainly adopts induction method to sum up a large number of cases, and extract the influencing factors and action paths related to fraudulent acts. However, with the passage of time and the change of society and culture, the behavior pattern of the actor will change, the research perspective of the researchers will continue to evolve accordingly, the explanatory power of the specific agent theory model will gradually weaken, and new models will constantly come out, which leads to the current situation that the current agent theories and models are in full bloom. Moreover, due to the lack of situational factors, its explanatory power has been gradually weakened in the increasingly complex analysis of financial fraud.

Research on Financial Fraud from the Perspective of Social Psychology

Social psychology is a branch of psychology that studies the social psychological phenomena of individuals or groups. The social psychological phenomena at the individual level mainly refer to the psychological phenomena that individuals are influenced by group factors in society, such as interpersonal perception, interpersonal attraction, social restraint and social compliance. Financial fraud from the perspective of social psychology, in a sense, can also be understood as the expansion of the crime motive theory. The traditional crime motive theory tends to attribute crime motive to some individual traits, whereas social psychology holds that it is far from enough to explain crime motive only to the extent of individual traits, since the formation of each person's traits is influenced by the social environment in which he lives (Carver & Scheier, 1982). To be concrete, because of relatively macroscopic social factors, social psychology is inclined to look for proxy variables to represent macro factors from the perspective of cultural and demographic features, and then explore the causes of financial fraud.

In terms of culture, the existing research can be further divided into social and cultural studies and corporate culture studies. Firstly, from the perspective of society and culture, an honest and open social and cultural atmosphere can effectively curb financial fraud (Huberts, 1998), while competitive social culture is highly likely to exacerbate the economic pressure of executives of listed companies and increase the motives for them to engage in financial fraud (Reinstein & Bayou, 1998). Secondly, from the perspective of corporate culture, a great many scholars have made attempts to explore financial fraud under different cultures. Furthermore, the impact of corporate culture on financial fraud is also reflected in three aspects of motive, opportunity and rationalization. In terms of motives, profit-oriented corporate culture is conducive to innovation and efficiency of enterprises, but such cultural value will also exert great pressure on the management, resulting in a strong motive for fraud (Messner & Rosenfeld, 2012). In terms of opportunity, the organizational culture with more centralized organizational authority will increase the decision-making power of the senior executives, and once the senior executives in the organization has the tendency to engage in fraud, fraudulent acts will gradually evolve into the unconscious behavior of the subordinates (Ashforth et al., 2008). In addition, if too much attention is paid to etiquette and prestige in culture, it is more likely to reduce the efficiency of organizational supervision, thereby leading to the prevalence of fraudulent acts (Jensen, 1993). As far as rationalization is concerned, collective decision-making tends to lead to the state of collective unconsciousness, so that it prefers to neglect the potential for fraud (Janis & Mann, 1977). The organizational culture that lays stress on human relationship will lower the fraudster's psychological pressure of morality and punishment, while increasing the risk of fraud (Kassem & Higson, 2012).

From the perspective of motive, the maturity of the actor is obviously related to the moral level, because the mature actor has experienced more, has a more thorough understanding of social norms and assumed a higher cost of criminal acts. In this regard, with the growth of age, managers are less likely to engage in financial fraud (Kelley, 1976). Besides, young managers prefer more to risk (Markoczy, 2001), so they tend to adopt more radical strategies in face of problems (Brouthers et al., 2002), which is also the intrinsic reason for the close relationship between age and financial fraud.

From the perspective of rationalization, Zahra et al. (2005) believe that the demographic characteristics of executives will also have an impact on the rationalization mechanism of the actor, which is because the demographic characteristics can better reflect the social status and social relations of the actor from the perspective of social psychology. Gross (2016) study found that key demographic characteristics, such as age, gender, experience and education level, provide a more effective way to predict fraudulent acts of executives. What's more, education level has a positive correlation with the moral level of the actor. The higher the moral level is, the more difficult it is to rationalize fraudulent acts. In this way, the higher educational level the actor has, the less likely it is for him or her to adopt fraudulent acts. In addition, In addition, position plays a similar role with age, as the disparity in position can better reflect the knowledge accumulation of managers. The higher position the manager holds, the richer experience and the wider knowledge he has, the more solutions there will be to problems (Kirton, 1976). Therefore, the possibility of solving problems with fraudulent acts will be declined accordingly.

To sum up, the study of financial fraud from the perspective of social psychology, similar to the study of crime motive theory, mainly explores the mechanism of the dependent variables of financial fraud by means of case induction, which is an effective way for us to have knowledge about the numerous factors that affect fraudulent acts, but there is no systematic framework to integrate these factors. Therefore, it is unable to analyze the mechanism of financial fraud in essence.

Research on Financial Fraud from the Perspective of Neoinstitutional Economics

The research on financial fraud from the perspective of neoinstitutional economics is mainly aimed at the analysis of institutional factors affecting financial fraud. Furthermore, the principal-agent theory is an important theoretical basis for the analysis of financial fraud from the perspective of neoinstitutional economics. As mentioned above, the governance mechanism in corporate governance can be divided into internal and external supervision mechanism.

Among them, the research on internal supervision mainly involves factors, such as the governance structure and the characteristics of board of directors, which will have an impact on financial fraud (Crutchley et al., 2007). In fact, many financial fraud cases are caused by the negligence of the board of directors and the board of supervisors (Dechow et al., 1996), the reasons for which are involved in the problems in both mechanism design and subjectivity. From the perspective of mechanism design, it will be easier for the CEO to control the board of directors with a large size and decentralized power. Especially when the CEO concurrently serves as the chairman of the board of directors, the board of directors will be less effective in supervision. In addition to the size of the board of directors, the size of shareholders also affects the efficiency of supervision. In the case of scattered shareholders and lack of substantial shareholders with strong discourse power, it is impossible to avoid fraud through supervision (Dechow et al., 1995). Besides, if the CEO is also the founder of the company, he will have a strong power, and not allow the idea of failure to occupy his mind, thereby increasing the probability that he will solve the difficulties by means of financial frauds. Secondly, the source of directors also has an impact on financial fraud. The more external directors the company has, the longer they hold their positions and the higher shareholding ratios they have, the less likely financial fraud will occur (Beasley, 1996). On the contrary, the more independent directors the board has, the more restrained the senior executives will be to commit financial frauds (Uzun et al., 2004). Thirdly, the shareholding ratio of the management and the design of stock options will also have an impact on financial fraud. In case that the managers hold a high proportion of stocks, managers will have strong motives to increase the company's stock price (Johnson et al., 1985), while it may also enhance the rationalization of senior executives for fraudulent acts (Troy et al., 2011). From a subjective point of view, independent directors are not omnipotent. In spite of high independence for external directors in judgment, they have been outside the company for a long time and paid limited attention to a specific company (Beasley, 1996). However, the governance of listed companies is extremely multifarious and disorderly, and then it is worth discussing whether independent directors can discover the well-designed fraud in this complex system with their limited energy (Bushman et al., 2004).

From the perspective of external governance, the traditional principal-agent theory believes that the independence of external auditors can effectively suppress financial fraud, but the independence of auditors is also affected by various factors. Generally speaking, auditors in large firms are more capable of keeping independent (DeAngelo, 1981), which is because large firms usually have a long history of business, and attach more importance to the brand and reputation, and thus they are less likely to violate their independence in order to fawn on very few clients or to win several high-profit contracts (Earley et al., 1990).

According to the above research, the characteristics of board of directors and governance structure will endow the specific decision makers with excessive power and authority under specific circumstances, which will greatly enhance the potential risk of financial fraud, while the external governance mechanism can make up for the deficiencies of internal governance mechanism to a certain extent. Generally speaking, financial fraud research from the perspective of neoinstitutional economics focuses on how to make use of the institutional or mechanism design to prevent fraudulent acts. In the final analysis, the analysis in this way still focuses on the motives, especially the in-depth excavation of the institutional factors in motives. It still does not jump out of the first two paradigms and lacks a systematic framework, while only the necessary conditions of financial fraud are expounded and the sufficient conditions fail to be explained.

Research on Financial Fraud from the Perspective of Economic Game Theory

The biggest difference between game theory and the perspectives mentioned above is that the cost-benefit analysis, a basic criterion of human behavior, is proposed. This analysis framework simplifies the analysis scenario of fraud problems, and sums up the cost, benefit and risk factors from the fraud problems on the basis of rational man. Then, the game model is constructed on this basis to infer the causes of fraudulent acts.

Wilks & Zimbelman (2004) found from the game model that financial fraud is mainly caused by material interests and less correlated with the level of individual morality.. However, this study ignores the role of regulators. Qin Jiangping and Duan Xingmin (2005) added the analysis of regulators on this basis, believing that the reason for the increasing financial fraud in China was that the regulators lacked incentives and failed to supervise the fraudulent acts of actors in an effective way, thus greatly reducing the cost of fraud. What's more, the collusion between listed companies and auditing agencies has made it more difficult for the regulators to supervise them (Chen & Zhang, 2008), which ultimately led to the emergence of financial frauds in an endless stream.

Based on the cost-benefit analysis, game theory eventually incorporates the influencing factors of financial fraud into a unified systematic analysis framework. Thus, all financial fraud problems can be abstracted into the analytical framework of antecedents, cost-benefit analysis and financial fraud, as well as the analysis of related intermediary and regulatory variables, thereby further opening up the way for the excavation of the necessary and sufficient conditions of financial fraud. However, the analysis of game theory is based on the hypothesis of rational man, which is still far from the real behavior of human beings. After all, the real actor has bounded rationality, and is affected by many psychological factors for making decisions. For this reason, the financial fraud research based on game theory has made more progress than the previous perspectives, but it is still unable to incorporate psychological factors into the analysis, making it unable to fully analyze every aspect of financial fraud.

Research on Financial Fraud from the Perspective of Prospect Theory

Prospect theory has integrated the theoretical perspectives mentioned above, which is based on the cost-benefit analysis in the economic game theory and the hypothesis that people refer to expectations to make decisions, thus optimizing the analytical framework of rational man in game theory. On this basis, relevant scholars have further introduced the crime motive theory and psychological variables in social psychology into cost-benefit analysis and principal-agent analysis based on prospect theory, which substantially increases the situational factors, thus making the mechanized analysis model closer to the real situation and effectively enhancing the explanatory power of the theory of the firm to reality. The analysis framework of prospect theory summarizes the achievements in previous studies as shown in Figure 1.

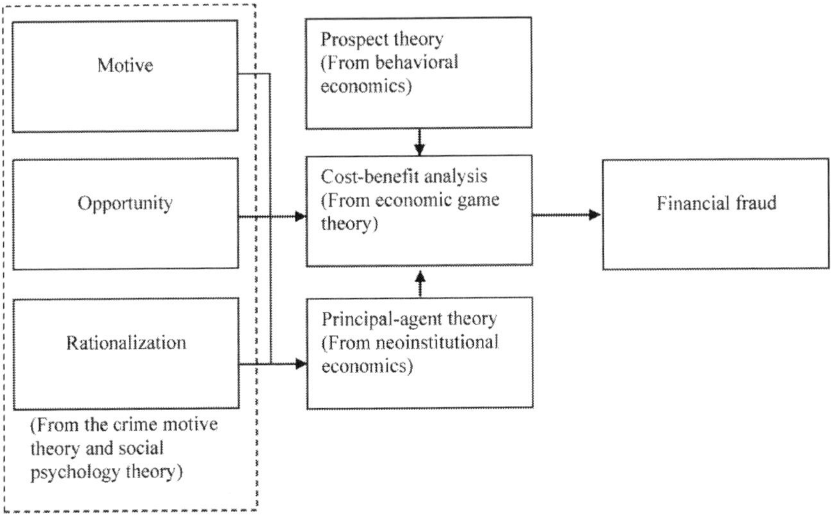

Figure 2-1 Analysis Framework of Financial Fraud under Prospect Theory

The prospect theory (Kahneman & Tversky, 1979) provides a basis for further analysis of the strategic adjustment behavior of enterprises. Pursuant to the theory, the enterprise, as a goal-oriented system, adopts simple decision rules to adjust the enterprise behavior based on performance feedback, which provides a preliminary criterion for decision makers to assess the current performance of the enterprise, to determine whether to seek for alternative solutions and whether to change the existing operating rules of the enterprise (Greve, 1998). Therefore, it is not difficult to understand that the performance goal of an enterprise is an important factor affecting the strategic behavior of decision makers. Unlike the traditional game theory analysis which merely regards the maximization of benefits or profits as the ultimate goal of decision-making, prospect theory holds that the effective and rational decision makers hardly make any optimal choice, while they make decisions mainly based on psychological satisfaction value as a reference point. At the organizational level, the reference point of an enterprise is mainly composed of the expected level of its operation. Decision makers of bounded rationality tend to make decisions for subsequent acts based on the gap between current actual performance and the expected level. In case that the actual performance is lower than the expected level, the decision maker will define such state below expectation as a state of loss. When the actual performance is higher than the expected level, the decision maker will define the state above expectation as a state of gain. Based on these two distinct operating conditions, the decision makers will adopt entirely different decision-making behaviors (Cyert & March, 1963).

According to this theory, when the actual performance is lower than the target expectation, the larger the gap is, the more difficult it will be for the organization to extricate itself from the state of loss, and then the more likely it will be to make decisions to take a risk:

Firstly, the gap between the actual performance and performance expectation represents that there are some problems in the organization in terms of resource allocation, internal management, production and manufacturing or marketing strategy, which urgently need to be adjusted to achieve transformation or change. The larger the gap from the expectation is, the more likely it is for managers to be aware of the problems in the organization, which will further prompt them to adopt strategic changes, such as exploring new techniques and making innovations, improving marketing strategies such as products, services and sales, withdrawing from or entering new markets, restructuring the structure and the system and updating the strategies (Grinyer & McKiernan, 1990).

Secondly, the legitimacy of the existence of enterprises decreases with the increase of the gap in the performance expectation, and the stakeholders have growing doubts about the necessity of the existence of the organization and the ability of managers. Especially when there is no effective solution to the continuous decline of corporate performance, the enterprise concerned will be forced to make a reasonable explanation for the continuous decline. In the meantime, shareholders and investors and other stakeholders will also enhance their concern and supervision of the enterprise with declining performance. When internal and external crises affect the legitimacy of an enterprise, it has to rethink about its own strategies so as to solve the internal organizational dilemma (Oliver, 1992). And the lower the performance is, the more intense pressure of strategic change it will trigger (Williamson & Ouchi, 1981).

Thirdly, the performance of the organization is closely bound up with the promotion opportunities and wage increases of the employees.

On the contrary, enterprises with poor performance will bring bad expectations to employees, such as salary cuts and layoffs, which may eventually lead to employees' voluntary departure. Once core employees leave office, it is likely to trigger more serious business problems. If the enterprise takes the initiative to adjust its strategy, it will enable its employees to believe that the enterprise is actively solving problems and that the dilemma will be the history.

Fourthly, the gap in performance expectations has an important impact on managers' reputation in the labor market. When the gap in performance expectations emerges, managers will be more motivated to rescue the organization by taking risks in order to maintain their bargaining power in future job-hopping (Baum & Dahlin, 2007). In addition, the gap in performance expectations also helps to the managers' mind of adhering to old habits, urge them to constantly reflect on and find problems in time, encourage them to search for information, and then constantly learn and adjust their strategic direction.

In a word, in face of performance decline, decision makers respond faster to threats than to opportunities, resulting in the low-performance organizations being required to do more to improve their performance, which leads to a number of risk-taking behaviors, such as technological innovation, product or service improvement, management system innovation, and strategic restructuring and so forth. Of course, it also includes negative risk-taking behavior, financial fraud. Furthermore, in the context of the increasing attention paid to the current external supervision mechanism, the managers have to attach increasing importance to the business pressure arising from the analysts' expectations. Therefore, from the perspective of prospect theory, this book will explore the relationship between performance pressure caused by the analysts' expectations and financial fraud in depth.

Table 2-1 Representative Studies on Financial Fraud

No.	Author	Theoretical perspective	Title	Research focus
1	Cressey(1950)	Criminology	The Criminal Violation of Financial Trust	It put forward three conditions of white-collar crime, which had ultimately evolved into the three elements of the fraud triangle theory after the continuous deliberations and development of later scholars, namely, perceived pressure, perceived opportunity and rationalization.
2	Albrecht et al.(2004)		Fraud & Corporate Executives: Agency, Stewardship & Broken Trust	It introduced the fraud triangle theory into the analysis of corporate financial affairs, and found that the more dignity and belief the managers have and the higher career satisfaction they pursue, the less likely it will be for them to engage in financial fraud.
3	Apostolou et al. (2016)		Accounting Education Literature Review (2015)	It elaborated on the pressure elements in the fraud triangle theory in depth, and believed that, besides the motives of fraud caused by subjective pressure, the objective pressure brought by higher authorities may also contribute to the fraudulent acts of subordinates.
4	Hermanson et al., (2006)		Continuous Monitoring of Transactions to Reduce Fraud, Misuse, & Errors	It discussed the prevention and supervision of fraudulent acts and argued that the individual traits of the fraudsters should also be incorporated into the analysis framework of the fraud triangle.

No.	Author	Theoretical perspective	Title	Research focus
5	Dorminey et al., (2012)		The Evolution of Fraud Theory	On the one hand, the fraudsters need to have the ability to identify the loopholes in governance and cover up their own fraud. On the other hand, they also need to be equipped mentally to cope with the risk of being exposed and punished at any time.
6	Brooks et al.(2005)		Detecting & Preventing the Financing of Terrorist Activities: A Role for Government Accountants	It was found that there are two types of fraudsters, accidental fraudsters and absolute fraudsters, among which the accidental fraudster weighs and balances carefully before committing fraud while the absolute fraudster tends to engage in fraud whenever it finds an opportunity.
7	Beasley & Hermanson (2006)		How Sales Executives Can Avoid Accounting Fraud Allegations	It was found that the accidental fraudster and the absolute fraudster can be transformed into each other, and that the accidental fraudster whose acts are not discovered or exposed for a long time is likely to become an absolute fraudster.
8	Kong & Yu (2015)		Formation Mechanism of Accounting Fraud: Research Perspective and Future Prospect	The fraud triangle theory was reviewed. Based on the prototype of the fraud triangle theory, the related expanding research of the fraud triangle theory was introduced.
9	Tunley (2011)		Uncovering the Iceberg: Mandating the measurement of fraud in the United Kingdom	The iceberg theory was constructed to distinguish the objective conditions and subjective motives of the occurrence of fraud, and it was emphasized that besides the institutional design, judging and exploring the weaknesses of human nature is also of great significance to the governance of fraudulent acts.

No.	Author	Theoretical perspective	Title	Research focus
10	Bologna(1993)		H&book on Corporate Fraud	On the basis of the fraud triangle theory, the G-O-N-E theory involving four factors was proposed, including greed, opportunity, need and exposure.
11	Pryor et al.(1996)		Risk Factors for Serious Infection During Treatment with Cyclophosphamide & High-Dose Corticosteroids for Systemic Lupus Erythematosus	The theory of fraud risk factors was proposed to divide the possible risks in fraudulent acts into special risk factors and common risk factors, among which common risk factors are mainly related to corporate governance, while special risk factors are related to individual factors.
12	Rezaee(2002)		Fraudulent financial reporting: Prevention & Detection	It argued that the occurrence of financial fraud was the result of five factors, namely, cooks, recipes, incentives, monitoring and end results.
13	Carver & Scheier (1982)	Social psychology	Control Theory: A Useful Conceptual Framework for Personality–Social, Clinical, & Health Psychology	It is far from enough to explain crime motive only to the extent of individual traits, since the formation of each person's traits is influenced by the social environment in which he lives.
14	(Huberts, 1998)		What Can be Done Against Public Corruption & Fraud: Expert Views on Strategies to Protect Public Integrity	From the perspective of society and culture, an honest and open social and cultural atmosphere can effectively curb financial fraud
15	(Reinstein & Bayou, 1998)		The New Auditing Standard on Fraud can Help Financial Institutions	Competitive social culture is likely to exacerbate the economic pressure on senior executives of listed companies and increase the motives for financial frauds.
16	(Messner &Rosenfeld, 2012)		Crime & the American Dream	The impact of corporate culture on financial fraud is also reflected in motive, opportunity and rationalization.

No.	Author	Theoretical perspective	Title	Research focus
17	(Ashforth et al., 2008)		Reviewing Organizational Corruption	The organizational culture with more centralized organizational authority will increase the decision-making power of the senior executives, and once the senior executives in the organization has the tendency to engage in fraud, fraudulent acts will gradually evolve into the unconscious behavior of the subordinates
18	(Jensen, 1993)		The Modern Industrial Revolution, Exit, & the Failure of Internal Control Systems	If too much attention is paid to etiquette and prestige in culture, it is more likely to reduce the efficiency of organizational supervision, thereby leading to the prevalence of fraudulent acts
19	(Janis & Mann, 1977)		Emergency Decision Making: a Theoretical Analysis of Responses to Disaster Warnings	The corporate culture that advocates collective decision-making tends to lead to the state of collective unconsciousness, which is inclined to neglect the potential of fraud.
20	(Kassem & Higson, 2012)		The New Fraud Triangle Model	The organizational culture that lays stress on human relationship will lower the fraudster's psychological pressure of morality and punishment, thereby increasing the risk of fraud.
21	(Gross, 2016)		Development of a Financial Decision-Making Self-Efficacy Measure for Older Adults	It was found that key demographic characteristics, such as age, gender, experience and educational level, can predict fraudulent acts of senior executives more effectively.

No.	Author	Theoretical perspective	Title	Research focus
22	(Kelley, 1976)		Accountants & Auditors vs. White Collar Crime	The maturity of the actor is obviously related to the moral level, because the mature actor has experienced more, has a more thorough understanding of social norms and assumed a higher cost of criminal acts. In this regard, with the growth of age, managers are less likely to engage in financial fraud.
23	(Markoczy, 2001)		Consensus Formation During Strategic Change	Young managers prefer more to risk and therefore are more likely to engage financial fraud.
24	(Brouthers et al., 2002)		Industrial Sector, Perceived Environmental Uncertainty & Entry Mode Strategy	Young managers are more inclined to adopt more radical strategies to cope with changes.
25	(Kirton, 1976)		Adaptors & Innovators: A Description & Measure.,	The higher position the manager holds, the richer experience and the wider knowledge he has, the more solutions there will be to problems (Kirton, 1976), and the less likely it will be to engage in financial fraud.
26	(Zahra et al., 2005)		The Antecedents & Consequences of Top Management Fraud.	The higher degree the senior executives have, the less likely they will be to adopt fraudulent acts.
27	(Crutchley et al., 2007)	Neoinstitutional economics	Climate for Scandal: Corporate Environments that Contribute to Accounting Fraud	The negligence of the board of directors and the board of supervisors is one of the main antecedents of financial fraud.
28	(Dechow et al., 1995)		Detecting Earnings Management	If the board of directors and shareholders are in large scale with relatively decentralized power, the CEO will own more centralized rights, which makes it impossible to avoid financial frauds by means of supervision.

No.	Author	Theoretical perspective	Title	Research focus
29	(Beasley, 1996)		An Empirical Analysis of the Relation Between the Board of Director Composition & Fraudulent financial reporting.	If the CEO is the founder of the company with centralized power, the probability of financial fraud will increase. On the contrary, if the company has more external directors with a long time in office, high shareholding ratios and decentralized power, the possibility of financial fraud will decline.
30	(Uzun et al., 2004)		Board Composition & Corporate Fraud	The more independent directors there are in the board, the more restrained the financial frauds of senior executives will be.
31	(Bushman et al., 2004)		Financial Accounting Information, Organizational Complexity & Corporate Governance Systems	The inhibitory effect of external directors on financial fraud depends on the efforts made by the director in the governance of the company.
32	(Johnson et al., 1985)		An Analysis of the Stock Price Reaction to Sudden Executive Deaths: Implications for the Managerial Labor Market.	When the managers hold a higher proportion of stocks, the management will be strongly motivated to increase the company's stock price, which will make it more likely to engage in financial fraud.
33	(Troy et al., 2011)		CEO Demographics & Accounting Fraud: Who is More Likely to Rationalize Illegal Acts?	When the managers hold a higher proportion of stocks, the rationalization of their fraudulent acts will be enhanced.

No.	Author	Theoretical perspective	Title	Research focus
34	(Earley et al., 1990)		Impact of Process & Outcome Feedback on the Relation of Goal Setting to Task Performance	Large firms are less likely to violate their independence in order to please some special clients or to win a few high-profit contracts, which is because large firms usually have a long history of business operations, and attach more importance to brand and reputation. Therefore, the external supervision of large auditor firms is conducive to preventing financial fraud.
35	(Wilks & Zimbelman, 2004)	Economic game theory	Using Game Theory & Strategic Reasoning Concepts to Prevent & Detect Fraud	Through the game model, it was found that financial fraud is mainly caused by material interests and less correlated with the level of individual morality.
36	(Qin & Duan, 2005)		Game Analysis of Accounting Fraud and Its Supervision in Enterprises	It was believed that the reason for the increasing financial fraud in China is the lack of incentives for regulators to effectively supervise fraudulent acts of actors, which greatly reduces the cost of fraud, and thus increases the relative benefits of fraud in a disguised way.
37	(Chen & Zhang, 2008)		Game Theory Study on the Governance of Financial Fraud in Listed Companies	The collusion between listed companies and auditing agencies further increases the supervision cost of regulators.
38	(Dalton et al., 2007)	Prospect theory	The Fundamental Agency Problem & Its Mitigation: Independence, Equity, & the Market for Corporate Control	Internal governance can reduce the information asymmetry inside and outside the company, thereby reducing the probability of financial fraud.

No.	Author	Theoretical perspective	Title	Research focus
39	(Shi et al., 2016)		Buying Bad Behavior: Tournament Incentives & Securities Class Action Lawsuits	External governance mechanisms, such as investor supervision and analysts' expectations, have become the focus of financial fraud research. In this study, it was found that the excessively strong external governance mechanism will make senior executives feel that they have lost the management autonomy, thereby enhancing the tendency to rationalize financial fraud.
40	(Goranova et al., 2010)		Owners on both Sides of the Deal: Mergers & Acquisitions & Overlapping Institutional Ownership	Researchers mainly focus on institutional investors, such as mutual funds, hedge funds, pension funds, banks, insurance companies and donors, and explore the impact mechanism of shareholders on the output of the company in case that the external governance mechanism is the owner of the enterprise.
41	(Porter, 1992)		Capital Choices: Changing the Way America Invests in Industry	A small number of investors who hold a large amount of corporate stock for a long time are highly capable of supervising financial frauds.
42	(Aguilera et al., 2015)		Connecting the Dots: Bringing External Corporate Governance into the Corporate Governance Puzzle.	It explored how stakeholders outside the organization can supervise managers.
43	(Deci & Ryan, 2000)		The "What"&"Why" of Goal Pursuits: Human Needs & the Self-Determination of Behavior.	Pressure from external governance will reduce managers' management autonomy, thereby reducing their internal motives for compliance with the laws and disciplines.

No.	Author	Theoretical perspective	Title	Research focus
44	(Davidoff, 2013)		A Push to End Securities Fraud Lawsuits Gains Momentum	External stakeholders are inclined to reduce the possibility that managers engage in financial frauds by enhancing their supervision and control.
45	Chen et al., (2006)		Ownership Structure, Corporate Governance, & Fraud: Evidence from China	The external governance mechanism based on supervision and self-discipline can effectively reduce the probability of financial fraud.
46	Lian et al. (2014)		The Performance Aspiration Gap and the Strategy Adjustment: A Case Study Based on China's Listed Companies	It analyses the relationship between the gap in performance expectations and strategic adjustment based on prospect theory, and explores the characteristics of the power subject, including the identity of controlling shareholder, the personality and source of CEO, as well as the regulatory role of resource endowment.
47	Lian (2015)		Performance Aspiration, Managerial Discretion and Strategic Change	Based on prospect theory and the upper echelons perspective, it focuses on the relationship between business expectation and strategic change, and explores the regulatory role of organizational, environmental and institutional autonomy of the managers on the relationship between the two.

Review of Influencing Factors of Financial Fraud

Internal Governance Mechanism and Financial Fraud of Enterprises

Ownership Structure and Corporate Financial Fraud

There are two main views on the relationship between ownership structure and corporate financial fraud. On the one hand, the higher the ownership concentration is, the more motivated shareholders will be to supervise the management in an effective way, thereby reducing the probability of financial fraud in the enterprise (Loebbecke & John, 1992). Especially with the increase of shareholding ratio of institutional investors, the probability of financial fraud in the enterprise will show a significant decline (Sharma, 2004; Vineeta. D. Sharma, 2004). In case of a relatively decentralized ownership structure, it can not form an effective supervision mechanism, and the scattered minority shareholders will be unable to monitor the opportunistic behavior of the management in an effective manner, which will lead to a higher probability of financial fraud (Dechow et al., 1996). On the other hand, related studies suggest that with the improvement of ownership concentration, the governance of the company may deteriorate, while increasing the possibility of financial fraud (La Porta, 1998; Cai et al., 2003; Liang et al., 2004; Liu & Du, 2003; Halioui & Chellouf, 2013). La Porta (1998) found that the higher the ownership concentration the company has and the lower the quality of financial statements is, the more likely it is to engage in fraud. Halioui & Chellouf (2013) found that ownership concentration was positively correlated with financial fraud. Liu Liguo and Du Ying (2003) argued that the higher the legal person shareholding ratio is, the more likely it is for the company to commit financial fraud, especially when the largest shareholder is SASAC (State-owned Assets Supervision and Administration Commission).

Board Size and Corporate Financial Fraud

At present, scholars at home and abroad have not reached a consensus on whether the board size will affect financial frauds of enterprises Beasley, 1996; Pfeffer & Salancik, 1978; Lipton & Lorsch, 1992; Monks & Minow, 1995; Dalton, 1999; Adams & Mehran, 2002; Cai & Liang, 2003; Persons, 2006, 2011; Zhang et al., 2006; Yang et al., 2009). Some scholars believe that with the expansion of the board size, the number of directors with various resources in hand will increase, which will lower the probability of the management controlling the board, while the increase in the number of directors in the board decreases the responsibilities that each director assumes, so that the directors will spend more time and energy monitoring the management, thus effectively reducing financial fraud (Pfeffer & Salancik, 1978; Monks & Minow, 1995; Adams & Mehran, 2002). However, some other scholars believe that the larger the board of directors is, the less clear the division of powers and responsibilities will be, and the more likely it is for the directors to shuffle responsibility onto each other, which may result in a decline in the actual efficiency of supervision over the management, thus creating opportunities for financial fraud (Lipton & Lorsch, 1992). In the meantime, the serious bureaucratism in large-scale boards of directors is also one of the important factors leading to financial fraud of managers (Beasley, 1996; Dalton, 1999; Shen & Zhang, 2002; Cai & Liang, 2003; Persons, 2006).

Independent Director and Corporate Financial Fraud

The introduction of independent directors can help to establish an effective mechanism of checks and balances and supervision in the board of directors, and it has been confirmed in a large number of previous documents that a high proportion of independent directors can effectively weaken the financial fraud of enterprises (Fama & Jensen, 1983; Loebbecke & John,1992; Beasley, 1996; Dwright ,1996; Beasley & Carcello, 2000; Liu & Du, 2003; Cai et al., 2003; Uzun, Szewczyk & Varma, 2004; Agrawal & Chadha, 2005; Farber, 2005, 2006; Persons, 2009; Chen, 2007; Wang, 2010; Halioui & Chellouf, 2013). Especially with the increase of the proportion of independent directors in audit committee, the possibility that the company engages in financial fraud will be further reduced (Cobb & Gordon, 1993; Uzun & Hatice, 2004; Persons, 2005). However, on the premise of a lower proportion of independent directors, it is more likely for the board of directors to be controlled and utilized by the management, and the deficiency in the corporate governance mechanism is the fundamental factor leading to financial fraud (Dechow, Sloan & Hutton, 1994; Beasley, 1996; Sweeney et al., 1996; Chen et al., 2006; Doyle, 2007; Wang & Sun, 2010; Bell & Carcello, 2011; Ettredge et al., 2011).

Audit Committee and Corporate Financial Fraud

The establishment of audit committee can strengthen the supervision of the board of directors to the managers, and identify the financial reporting problems of the company more effectively (Forker, 1992). Moreover, the establishment of audit committee helps to reduce the probability of financial fraud of the management (Loebbecke & John, 1992; Abbott & Park, 2004). In companies where an audit committee is seldom established, financial fraud is more likely to occur (Beasley, 2000; Dechow et al., 1996; Abbott & Park, 2004), because their internal auditing systems are less perfect (Beasley, 2000). With the deepening of research, scholars have further analyzed the impact of audit committee's composition characteristics and operation mechanism on financial frauds (Abbott et al., 2002; Persons, 2009; Persons, 2005; Farber, 2006), believing that the stronger the independence of the audit committee in an enterprise is (the higher the proportion of external directors is), the more professional it is (the higher the proportion of financial experts is), and the more diligent the audit committee is (the more frequently the meetings are held), the more conducive it will be to urging the management to adopt more robust and legitimate accounting methods and policies (Susan et al., 1997), thus effectively reducing the probability of financial fraud (Abbott et al., 2002; Persons, 2005; Persons, 2009; Farber, 2005; Farber, 2006). However, some scholars believe that the establishment and independence of the audit committee do not have a significant impact on the incidence of financial fraud among managers (Beasley, 1996; Yang et al., 2009).

External Governance Mechanism and Financial Fraud of Enterprises

Institutional Supervision and Financial Fraud

Due to active and effective supervision and punishment by the CSRC (China Securities Regulatory Commission) and the exchanges, the listed companies violating regulations will be faced with serious economic consequences (Chen et al., 2005; Liebman & Mihaupt, 2008; Xin et al., 2013), which reflects that improving the supervision efficiency of the regulators can reduce the incidence of financial frauds for enterprises (Dyck et al., 2010). Chen Jiasheng (2014) found that the supervision efficiency of related government departments has a significant negative correlation with the sustainability of financial fraud of listed companies, and that the more timely and effectively the supervision department intervenes in financial fraud, the less likely the listed companies will engage in continuous financial frauds. Dyck et al. (2010) found that the supervision efficiency of industry-related regulators also has a significant negative correlation with the probability of financial fraud of listed companies. Zhang Ran et al. (2015) found that the receipt of corporate announcement comment letter disclosed publicly by the Securities and Exchange Commission (SEC) played a significant role in predicting the financial frauds of the companies, and that compared to the enterprises that did not receive the comment letter from the SEC, those that received the letter were more likely to engage in financial fraud in the future. The more problems the SEC comment letter posed, the more likely the company would engage in financial frauds in the future. Moreover, the research of Chen & Johnston (2008) and Johnston & Petacchi (2013) found that when the company solved the problems posed by the SEC comment letter, the accounting information environment of the company would be significantly improved, and the quality of accounting information could be effectively improved accordingly.

Media Supervision and Financial Fraud

In addition to the supervision of traditional supervisory bodies, the supervision of other non-traditional market participants, such as employees, customers, especially the news media, is also an important mechanism to effectively suppress the occurrence of financial frauds in enterprises (Dyck et al., 2010). Miller (2006) studied the supervisory role of the news media in reducing and discovering fraudulent acts, and found that the stronger supervision the media implements and the more attention an enterprise attracts from the media, the less likely it will be for the enterprise to commit financial frauds. In addition, studies have found that the larger the company suspected of being involved in fraud and the more people it is involved in, the more likely it will be for the news media to report fraudulent acts of such company.

Internal Business Distress and Financial Fraud of Enterprises

At present, scholars at home and abroad have not reached a consensus on whether there is a close relationship between business distress and financial fraud within the enterprises (Treadway Committee, 1987; Kinney & McDanie, 1989; Aquila, 1998; Howe, 1999; Bell & carcello, 2000; Pankaj, 2001; Chen, 2005; Li, 2002; Chen & Wang, 2005; Lara-Hoffmans, 2010). However, most of the scholars believe that there is a close relationship between business distress and financial fraud within the enterprises, which means that internal business distress may easily give rise to financial frauds in enterprises (Treadway & Committee, 1987; Kinney & McDanie, 1989; Bell & carcello, 2000; Chen & Wang, 2005), which is mainly because internal business distress will pose tremendous operating pressure to enterprises, and even affect the listing and allotment of stocks (Li, 2002). In addition, the management is more prone to financial fraud in order to achieve higher returns than actual performance (Howe, 1999), cater to the expected earnings targets and complete operating performance (Lara-Hoffmans, 2010), conceal temporary financial difficulties (Kinney & McDanie, 1989; Lara-Hoffmans, 2010), as well as avoid penalties (Li, 2002), and even to be free from the threat of bankruptcy (Pankaj, 2001). On the contrary, better internal operating conditions are conducive to restraining financial fraud of listed companies (Bell & Carcello, 2000; Chen, 2005), while a small number of scholars hold that the pressure of performance and code of conduct of the enterprise to its management does not have a significant impact on financial fraud (Aquila, 1998).

Personality Traits and Financial Fraud of Senior Executives

Since the organization theory was first proposed, senior executives are one of the necessary components (Barnard, 1938; Chandler, 1962). In the Harvard School, senior managers even play a key role in shaping the organization (Andrews, 1971). Cyert and Arch (1963) coined the concept of dominant coalition, while Child (1972) further pointed out that the dominant coalition in a particular period determined the choice of strategy. However, before the 1980s, organizational researchers had paid more attention to technological and economic factors, but less to human factors. Even when the strategic process was studied in depth, scholars still concentrated on the transmission of information and decision-making, and stripped human factors (Aguilar, 1967; Allen, 1979; Bourgeois, 1980; Mintzberg et al., 1976). As Finkelstein and Hambrick (1996) pointed out, there was a lack of relevant research on the dominant coalition, which was radically because the academic circles had been lacking in a pioneering and systematic research since Child (1972).

What Effective General Managers Really Do, a book by John P. Kotter (1982), and Upper Echelons: The Organization as a Reflection of Its Top Managers, an article by Hambrick, D.C. and Mason, P.A. (1984), opened up new fields for the research on senior executives and organizational impact in academic circles. The former assumes that the disparity in managers' behavior can be attributed to their individual background characteristics, while the latter proposes a rigorous academic research framework, which is known as the upper echelons perspective believing that the strategic choice of an organization is based on the cognitive basis, values and other inner psychological characteristics of senior executives. In the three aspects of vision (which direction to look or listen), selective perception (what to see or hear) and interpretation, the internal and external environmental information received is screened and filtered, and finally a strategic decision with obvious personal style is developed, which shapes the output of the organization. Since these two works, theoretical and empirical studies on the impact of senior executives' background characteristics on the strategic decision-making and performance of the organizations have begun to grow exponentially.

To analyze the top managers, the theoretical framework is based on three important points of view. Firstly, one of the focuses of macroscopic organization research is dominant coalition, or senior executives. As a strategic decision maker of an organization, senior executives are confronted with a very complex situation, which is far beyond their comprehension, and thus they tend to make decisions based on their cognitive basis and values. In order to better understand the operation of an organization, it is necessary to analyze the characteristics of its senior executives, because to some extent, the characteristics of senior executives determine the strategic choice, which further determines the performance of the organization. Secondly, compared with single senior executives, the overall research and analysis of top management team can more accurately predict the organization's output (strategic decision-making or performance), which is because the CEO tends to assign its power and tasks to the entire top management team, and any factors affecting individual decision choices will affect the organization's decision-making and performance in the form of team heterogeneity. Thirdly, demographic characteristics that are easily measured can be used in empirical research to replace psychological characteristics that are difficult to measure, such as values and cognitive basis. Hambrick and Mason (1984) and Finkelstein and Hambrick (1997) elaborated on two types of personal characteristics, psychological factors and demographic characteristics (observable experience), among which the former is clearly constructed but difficult to measure, while the latter reduces the difficulty of measurement but tends to be vulnerable to potential psychological factors. Therefore, the two coexist in the upper echelons perspective, and the authors also propose the relationship between experience and psychological factors, including context, characteristics of senior executives, strategic choice and organizational performance.

During the ten years after the emergence of the upper echelons perspective, a great deal of academic research boosted the development of this theory, but many defects were discovered at the same time. In many studies, the demographic characteristics of the top management team are regarded as the proxy variables of psychological characteristics, which confirm its impact on enterprise's strategic decision-making and performance. However, the conclusions vary from each other, and thus the scholars focus on the black box of the operating process of the top management team. Hambrick (1994) further promoted the development of the upper echelons perspective and proposed the concept of behavioral integration, which further uncovered the black box of the operating process of the top management team. What's more, he found that the research on the interaction and integration of senior executives' behavior helps to better illustrate the direct or indirect connection between the top management team and the strategic decision-making and performance of organizations. As Hambrick (2007) stated, the mysterious black box is the process of transforming the psychological and social activities of the top management team into strategic choices, and it is not just an academic study to unlock the black box, which is of extremely great help for the top management team to overcome prejudices caused by experience and personality. For example, it is usually more difficult for senior executives who serve for a long time to make flexible adjustments, but it is not certain actually.

It is because they need a larger number of clearer evidence to gain insight into new trends, and there are some other reasons (Hambrick & Fukutomi, 1991; Henderson et al., 2006). The concept of behavior integration originated from Hambrick's finding that in many top management teams, senior executives have a bilateral relationship with the CEOs but have little contact with other members, so that he proposed the concept of behavior integration to represent to what extent the top management team makes multilateral and collective interaction. Hambrick et al. (1996) gave a more detailed and standardized description of the operating process of the top management team from the perspective of its heterogeneity. In fact, it has been proved in subsequent studies that behavioral integration is directly and positively related to organizational performance (Hambrick, 1998; Li & Hambrick, 2005; Lubatkin et al., 2006). With the further study of the upper echelons perspective, the development of regulatory and mediating variables has made the research more refined (Hambrick, 2007; Bube et al., 2011), in addition to exploring more demographic features and expanding the operating process of the team (Amason & Sapienza, 1996; Athanassiou & Nigh, 2002; Bunderson & Sutcliffe, 2002; Carpenter, 2002; Finkelstein & Hambrick, 1996).

After reviewing the studies based on the upper echelons perspective by Hambrick and Mason (1984), Carpenter et al. (2004) pointed out that the upper echelons perspective model established its validity several years after its birth, and then the research for nearly twenty years greatly strengthened its universality, and that the impact of senior executives on organizations can be found everywhere, whether in the domestic or international community, mature enterprises or start-ups, profit-oriented institutions or public institutions. In addition, a large number of research results not only expand the original strategic scope to the international community, but it is also found that the governance environment and internal psychological factors of the top management team are still equipped with the explanatory power, when the demographic characteristics of senior executives can not explain the new decision choices. Another important finding is that the interactive processes in the operation of the top management team, such as communications and debates, also exert an impact on the decision choice. Interactive process can be used as an independent mechanism and ultimately affect the performance of the organization, which can also regulate the relationship between the demographic characteristics of the top management team and its strategic choice in some cases. After integrating a large number of recent advances in the study of the upper echelons perspective, Carpenter et al. (2004) proposed the third generation of the upper echelons perspective model, which was based on the integration of the former upper echelons perspective and agent theory, since the upper echelons perspective holds that the feature of the top management team is the predictive variable of organizational performance, but neglect the governance environment of senior managers, while the agent theory pays more attention to analyzing the governance environment of organizations, but neglects the disparity between demographic characteristics and psychological factors of senior executives. In view of this, by incorporating the two theories into an analytical framework, it can better analyze the relationship between top management team and the strategic decision-making and performance of organizations. The model adds pre-variables of internal organization and external environment of the top management team's characteristics to construct a new theory of top management team's characteristics. In addition, five intermediary and regulatory variables are proposed to explain the influence mechanism between the characteristics of the top management team and the output of the organization, so as to make the upper echelons perspective more comprehensive.

Carpenter et al. (2004) summarized three aspects strengthened on the basis of the former upper echelons perspective, including testing the direct impact of senior executives on corporate output, exploring the influence of the composition of the top management team on its internal interaction and decision-making process, and emphasizing the importance of internal and external environment, namely, the impact of the characteristics of senior executives on the formation of corporate strategy and organizational performance. Carpenter et al. ((2004) also pointed out that it has become a new trend to apply the upper echelons perspective to the field of international research (Carpenter et al., 2001; Reuber & Fischer, 1997; Sambharya, 1996). In the new field of interdisciplinary research, nationality or the experience of international life, learning and work represent the background characteristics that can be observed. Through the psychological study of the above observable characteristics, it is pointed out that foreigners can introduce different values, cognitive styles and personality traits to the top management team, while the local senior executives with international experience also enable the enterprises to acquire various knowledge of the market overseas. For this reason, the top management team with international background means corresponding values, cognitive patterns and other knowledge of the market overseas. According to theory and logic, the international professional knowledge in this case will propel the top management team in international enterprises to perform their duties, while the research applied in the field of enterprise internationalization has injected fresh blood into the development of the upper echelons perspective, and also confirmed the significance of the top management team for international enterprises. As the international start-ups have been frequently established in recent years, the studies that introduce the upper echelons perspective into the emerging international start-ups will give new impetus to the development of the two.

From the perspective of social psychology, the study mainly explains the causes of financial fraud based on demographic characteristics, psychological or personality factors, believing that the demographic characteristics and personality and psychological characteristics of senior executives affect the implementation of their financial fraud to a large extent (Hambrick & Mason, 1984; Li et al., 2002; Zhu & Gao, 2007; Zahra et al., 2007; Demerjian et al., 2013; Aier et al., 2015; Zhou et al., 2016; Zhou et al., 2017).

Firstly, in terms of the demographic characteristics of senior executives, the age of senior executives represents their own experience, and the older the senior executives are, the more sensitive they will be to the risk, and the higher demand for the quality of financial statements there will be (Huang et al, 2012), and they are less likely to engage in financial fraud (Hambrick & Mason, 1984). However, the learning experience of senior executives is highly correlated with the knowledge they acquire about economic management. Aieret et al. (2015) found that the CFOs with better expertise, such as academic qualifications, professional qualifications and so forth, would reduce financial restatements of enterprises. In addition, Zhou Kaitang et al. (2017)

pointed out that senior executives with academic experience would be more conservative and strive for the stability of accounting information and reduce their own motives for earnings management. However, Dechow et al. (1996) found that the experience of managers who study for MBA enables them to attach more importance to the self-interest behavior, which is more likely to be involved in the accounting fraudulent acts of enterprises. In addition, the gender of senior executives has a profound impact on their engagement in financial frauds. Zhou Zejiang et al. (2016) found that female CEOs are more likely to engage in financial fraud, but they will suppress such behavior.

Age, which usually represents a person's experience, is not only related to the potential for his or her career development, but also affects the level of his or her risk preference, risk-bearing capacity and bounded rationality. Young managers are generally active in thinking and bold in innovation, while older managers are more fettered by old conventions. Hambrick et al. (1984) pointed out that part of managers' cognitive ability and flexibility decreased with age. Wiersema et al. (1992) found that older managers tended to avoid risks in order to keep a favorable position since they had accumulated their performance in the earlier days of their work. He Weifeng et al. (2010) also believed that older managers did not intend to pay for the adverse consequences of financial restatement, and thus they seldom adopted radical accounting policies so as to prevent the companies from financial restatement. Financial fraud is an opportunistic act. Through empirical research, Chen Yan et al. (2014) found that fraud tendencies of actors showed a downward trend with the age. Kong Chen et al. (2015) analyzed Kelly's view on the relationship between the maturity of the actor and the moral level and believed that the actors would have richer experience and much maturer ideas with the age, and that the managers would be more willing to believe that it took a huge cost to rationalize the excuses for financial frauds, while the young senior executives were more inclined to engage in fraudulent acts. In the context of profound Confucianism in China, the respect for seniority has been deeply rooted in the minds of the Chinese people, while the emotional factors that are keen on face-saving and dignity also have an important impact on work. Choi (2007) pointed out that in Eastern society, age is closely bound up with the stage of career development, and that it is likely for the young CEOs to cause other senior executives to have negative emotions such as inferiority.

Educational background reflects the level of education, which is closely related to the cultivation of a person's values, knowledge, skills and rationality. According to cognitive theory, the experience that a person receives education has a significantly positive correlation with his or her cognitive ability. Moreover, the educational level has been proved to be positively correlated with the moral level of the actor, as the higher the educational level is, the stronger the comprehensive thinking ability will be and the better the information processing capacity will be. When making decisions, the actor will carefully weigh the gains and losses as well as the advantages and disadvantages, evaluate and take into account these factors in a scientific and comprehensive way, while tending to avoid risk on their own initiative. Jiang Fuxiu et al. (2009) also found that academic qualifications have an impact on managers' rationality in decision-making, and the well-educated people seldom make excessive investments. Wiersema et al. (1992) pointed out that the higher the educational level of managers is, the more resources and support they will obtain from their social relations. Tihan et al. (2000) demonstrated that the better educated the senior executives are, the more complex their cognition will be due to the education they receive, and the higher prestige they will gain in the organization.

Generally speaking, attitudes towards risk preference and risk perceptions will vary by gender. Women tend to be sound and conservative, while men tend to be aggressive and risk-taking, and thus female managers usually have lower risk preferences than male managers. For events with the same uncertainties, men will take an active part in them as they are keen on challenging themselves, but woman are less willing to participate due to their fear of risk. Guo Minhua et al. (2005) found that men are more active than women to make investments and intend to do that in their minds, and that moral beliefs and rationality also vary greatly by gender. Meyers Levy (1989) proposed that women are more complex and delicate in information processing than men, and they need more arguments so as to develop affirmative cognition, while men tend to process information in a simple manner. Peng and Wei (2007) found that, by contrast, women are more cautious, while men are more likely to be over-confident in some aspects, and thus more prone to make wrong decisions. Krishnan and Parsons (2008) analyzed the world's top 500 companies on Fortune and found that female senior executives significantly improved the earnings quality of the company. Through empirical research, Chen Yan et al. (2014) found that the risk preference of the actor has a stable and significant positive correlation with fraud tendency, and that the level of over-confidence also has a significant positive correlation with fraud tendency.

Secondly, in terms of the personality and psychological characteristics of senior executives, the moral level of managers themselves is an important factor affecting their engagement in financial fraud (Aquila, 1998). Especially when the management has the records of dishonesty, fraud and evasion of responsibility, it will increase the possibility that they commit financial fraud (Loebbecke & Willingham, 1988). Furthermore, the greed of the management has also prompted them to gain their own benefits by means of financial fraud (Romney, 2008; Hong et al., 2012; Zhu & Gao, 2007). The senior executives who are over-confident, arrogant and arbitrary are generally directly related to early warning indicators of enterprises (Albrecht & Romney, 1986; Qin, 2005), but they often cover it up by consciously publishing overly optimistic misinformation thus significantly promoting financial fraud (Schron & Zechman, 2012).

In addition, managers' risk preferences exert a positive impact on their motives and tendencies to engage in financial fraud (Bruner et al., 2008; Hong et al., 2012). Relatively, the more capable managers are, the less likely the company will be to commit financial fraud and the higher the quality of accounting information will be (Demerjian et al, 2013).

Incentives and Power of Senior Executives and Financial Fraud

Incentives of Senior Executives and Corporate Financial Fraud

Current scholars have not reached a consensus on the relationship between senior executive incentives and corporate financial fraud. Some scholars believe that senior executives' shareholding plays a role in inhibiting financial fraud (Wang & Sun, 2010), and if managers are given reasonable incentives, corporate financial fraud can be prevented, which means that financial fraud occurs less likely (Liang et al., 2004; Beasley, 1996). Warfield et al. (1995) found that with the increase of the shareholding ratio of managers or investment institutions, the agency cost of enterprises decreases and the possible profit manipulation is restrained. It is precisely because the shareholding of the management makes the interests of shareholders consistent with those of the management that the management will take cautious attitudes towards the act that damages the value of the enterprise, thus decreasing the probability of financial fraud. However, some scholars believe that there is no obvious connection between the shareholding of senior executives and financial fraud in the fierce market competition (Yuan et al., 2007), and that the shareholding of the management does not reduce the probability of financial fraud (Erickson et al., 2006). Some other scholars believe that when the financial problems of the enterprise occur, equity incentives can stimulate managers' efforts, but they also increase the fraudulent tendency of the management, such as the temptation of arbitrage in the stock market (Adergassen, 2010), the pressure from the CFO (Feng et al., 2011), and the growing possibility of financial fraud in enterprises (Bruner, 2008; Burne et al., 2005; Johnson, 2006; Robison & Santore, 2006). The more sensitive the CEO's options to stock price are, the greater the possibility of financial information misstatement will be (Burns & Kedia, 2006).

Power of Senior Executives and Corporate Financial Fraud

As for the power of senior executives, some scholars point out that if the general manager serves concurrently as the chairman, namely, duality of general manager, the internal control system of the company will not play an effective role, thus reducing the supervision effect of the board of directors and increasing the probability of fraud in the company (Farber, 2006; Fama & Jensen, 1983; Agrawal & Chadha, 2005). Even, in many cases, duality is more likely to be intentionally done by the management to facilitate its fraud (Beasley, 1996). Thus, the more independent the board of directors is from the general manager, the more effectively the financial behavior of the enterprise can be monitored, thus reducing the probability of fraud (Abbotet et al., 2003; Klein, 2002). However, some scholars believe that duality gives the general manager greater decision-making power, which enables them to help the company respond more quickly to the dynamic and complex environment, objectively promotes the company to conduct R&D innovation and exploration of new areas, improves decision-making efficiency, and thus contributes to getting the company out of the difficulties through the improvement of actual performance, rather than financial fraud (Donaldson & Davis, 1991).

Performance Feedback and Financial Fraud

The performance feedback theory, as one of the main components of the prospect theory, emphasizes that managers established expected goals for performance, and defines the established expected goals as the minimum acceptance criteria for decision-making results. It is also the main reference point for performance evaluation. Moreover, the performance feedback theory takes the deviation between actual results and expected goals as the basis for subsequent risk decision-making. When the performance of an organization is higher than its expected goal, managers are more confident and capable of undertaking the risk, and high-performance organizations are usually equipped with more resources and capabilities to support the organization to invest resources, funds and engage in risky investment activities (Greve, 2003). But avoiding uncertainty is a basic hypothesis of prospect theory. When the performance of an organization is higher than its expected goal, managers may maintain their existing decisions and hold relatively conservative attitudes towards investment activities in order to reduce uncertainty. In practice, high performance enables the enterprise to engage in more risk-taking activities, but managers are likely to choose to maintain the original strategy in order to avoid uncertainty.

One of the core viewpoints of the performance feedback theory is that decision makers regard the expected level as an objective dimension for evaluating the performance of the organization, which allows the decision makers with bounded rationality to simplify performance evaluation as success or failure (March, 1988; March & Simon, 1958). The expected level is the core concept of the performance feedback theory. Once the expected level is established, the comparison with actual performance will lead to the process of organizational change, while the expected level is derived from performance learning of individuals, from other people's performance learning, or from direct learning of other people's expectations (Lewin et al., 1944). The expected level affects direct behavioral outcomes, such as risk-taking or innovation and other outcome variables. It is generally believed that the expected level of performance arises from the social comparison and the comparison of historical performance (Greve, 1998; Levinthal et al., 1981). Goal satisfaction is a function of the comparison with the same group or / and the level of early performance. Because organizations are susceptible to short-sightedness, they tend to rely on short-term performance feedbacks while neglecting the future situations (Levinthal & March, 1993). Moreover, there are often conscious or unconscious deviations in the future expectations of organizations (Cyert & March, 1963), and thus the future status is involved in too many uncertainties and deviations, making it seem less important to look forward. Current studies generally describe an organization as a backward-looking model (Chen, 2008), in which an organization compares its operating performance with its historical performance level and then makes gradual adjustments. On the other hand, social comparison is also a powerful factor in evaluating people's abilities and outcomes, which means that people tend to compare themselves with others like them (Miller & Prentice, 1996). The performance level of a reference organization or the same group is a benchmark for decision makers to evaluate their current performance. In the management-related literature, the expected level of social goals is modeled as the average performance of other enterprises in the industry or social network (Baum et al., 2005), but the literatures concerning organizational behavior tend to use more explicit measurement tools from the perceptible perspectives of individuals (Goodman & Haisley, 2007), such as similar age, sex, religious beliefs, educational background and so forth.

Performance feedback provides an important reference model for the decision-making of enterprise organizations, that is, how is the business situation of the enterprise now? Is it necessary to explore other ways and adjust the rules (Greve, 1998, 2003b; Lant, 1992)? Enterprises tend to make flexible adjustments based on past experience (Cyert & March, 1963), and these adjustments advance step by step, since organizations tend to make minor adjustments in the face of difficulties to test the effectiveness of new solutions (Quinn, 1978). Some scholars believe that when an organization fails to achieve its expected level of performance, it will lead to exploratory research and development, which, as a dilemma-driven goal, is to quickly solve the current problems to ensure that the performance can return to the expected level. But when enterprises achieve their goal expectations, they tend to maintain the existing rules and are seldom motivated to explore new approaches (Cyert & March, 1963; Levinthal & March, 1981). The behavioral perspective of enterprises is the main theoretical perspective for studying organizational risk or change, and the core hypothesis is that decision makers evaluate performance according to the expected level and that the gap between performance and the expected level affects their risk-taking and the direction for strategic change (Cyert & March, 1963; March & Shapira, 1987, 1992), which is mainly based on the psychological process of risk perception and preference. Most studies using this theoretical perspective show that performance improvements will reduce risk-taking when the performance is higher than the expected level, and that the impact of performance change on risk-taking is still in dispute when the performance is lower than the expected level. There are two opposing hypotheses, one is that performance is lower than the expected level, which stimulates the need for performance improvement and then provokes risk-taking behavior (Cyert & March, 1963; Kahneman & Tversky, 1979), while the other is that performance lower than the expected level highlights the danger signal, which will lead to risk aversion (Lopes, 1987; Sitkin & Pablo, 1992; Staw et al., 1981).

Forms of Corporate Financial Fraud in China

Common Forms of Corporate Financial Fraud

False Income Increase

The first is fictitious trånsaction and forged certificates. The main purpose of financial fraud is to increase the profit data. Therefore, it has become one of the important ways to increase income by means of fictitious transaction. The main methods of false income increase are forged transaction contracts, false invoices, forged delivery orders and so forth. As a result, although the accounting materials are complete, the operating income and profit of the enterprise are not really realized, and the enterprise does not obtain any actual income, but also needs to pay part of the tax corresponding to the false income increase. For the false increase of income, enterprises often take it as one of the items for accounts receivable, and finally classify it into the bad debt provision.

Moreover, companies are willing to bear such losses in order to achieve IPO listing, but financial fraud is likely to enable the companies to achieve the purpose of increasing false shares and raising stock prices. The second is illegal revenue confirmation. In order to increase false income, enterprises engaged in financial fraud can confirm their income by three illegal ways. One is that the sales contract clearly stipulates that the buyer can refund, but the enterprise confirms the sales revenue before the expiration of the refund period, and the other is that the income is confirmed in advance against the regulations. In addition, enterprises also adopt other unreasonable means of income confirmation to increase false income. The third is the related party transactions. The enterprises engaged in financial fraud often increase false income by means of related party transactions, as these enterprises can increase their operating income by constantly trading with the associated enterprises. In this process, these enterprises an also make the related party transactions less fair and equitable by means of negotiated pricing, thereby increasing their false income and profits.

False Increase in Assets and Owner's Equity

Firstly, it is the false increase of bank deposits. The financial fraud of enterprises by increasing bank deposits can be divided into two categories. One is that financial enterprises lend deposits to enterprises, and enterprises receiving loans re-deposit funds into financial enterprises so as to achieve a false increase in bank deposits. The other is that non-financial enterprises increase bank deposits by forged certificates and fictitious accounts receivable collected. An enterprise can easily achieve a false increase in its bank deposits in a few simple steps, in which the enterprise needs to pay part of the interest, but it can obtain a large number of funds and achieve the purpose of whitewashing financial statements. Secondly, it is the false increase of fixed assets, construction in progress or intangible assets. One way is to include the income from the change of fair value or investment income into the items of fixed assets or construction in progress in violation, the other way is to fictionalize the investment funds as fixed assets or construction in progress when they are not recovered, and yet another way is to achieve a false increase in fixed assets or construction in progress by way of depreciation not calculated in accordance with the prescribed method.

Thirdly, it is the false increase in investment. In order to expand the scale of assets in financial statements to better reflect profitability, enterprises will also shift the direction of financial fraud to false increase in investments. Common methods include false increase in the scale of long-term equity investment by false bank draft, amortization of balance of the long-term equity investment not according to regulations, and fictitious investment through external accounts.

False Decrease in Costs and Expenses

In order to increase profits, enterprises tend to make false increase in costs and expenses in addition to false income increase.

False Debt Decrease

Listed companies via IPO engage in financial frauds through false decrease in their debts, mainly by disclosing liabilities not according to regulations, including other payables in capital reserve, and including accounts payable in prepaid accounts.

Related Party Transactions

In some financial fraud cases of IPO listed companies, related party transaction is one of the important approaches.

Other Methods

First, it fails to disclose relevant information on fund-raising in accordance with regulations. The main methods include forging or changing the use of funds without permission, forging the scale of projects related to funds, and failing to disclose the restriction and disposal information of rights such as freezing and deducting funds according to regulations. Second, listed companies and directors, supervisors and executives of their affiliated parties engage in illegal trading of stocks and securities. To be concrete, directors, supervisors and executives of listed companies take advantage of other legal entities under actual control to trade stocks and securities of listed companies after having knowledge about the inside information, thus affecting the profits of such companies. Besides, the transactions of the substantial shareholders or directors, supervisors of listed companies on the stocks of the companies are not disclosed in accordance with regulations. Third, major transactions are not disclosed in accordance with the regulations.

In the process of financial fraud, the main ways to conceal major transactions are to fill the major transactions in the items of other receivables or other payables, or to disclose part information apparently but not to disclose the information of major transactions in accordance with regulations.

Typical Cases of Financial Fraud in China's Listed Companies

Financial Fraud Case by Chalkis

Founded in May 1992, Chalkis Health Industry Co., Ltd. (hereinafter referred to as "Chalkis"), was listed on the Shenzhen Stock Exchange on September 26, 2000. According to the financial statements provided by Chalkis, the total purchase amount of the top five customers in 2005 was 401 million Yuan, accounting for 38.96% of the total annual sales of Chalkis. However, in 2006, the cumulative sales of Chalkis to the top five customers increased to 1.04 billion Yuan, accounting for 58.35% of the total annual sales of Chalkis. In fact, the price of tomato market was stable in 2006, but the amount of products sold by Chalkis to the top five customers increased by more than 2.5 times in only one year, which had to surprise the public and regulators. Chalkis engaged in a serious financial fraud through the investigation of China Securities Regulatory Commission, which had constantly made false increase in its profits by means of false increases in its main business income from 2006 to 2011. In 2006, Chalkis funded Tianjin Shengzhong International Trade Co., Ltd. (hereinafter referred to as "Tianjin Shengzhong") in a more covert way at the behest of Chairman Liu Yi. On the surface, Tianjin Shengzhong was not associated with Chalkis, but the former was actually controlled by Chalkis. After the establishment of Tianjin Shengzhong, Chalkis sold tomato ketchup to Tianjin Shengzhong, and then Tianjin Shengzhong sold tomato ketchup to Tianjin Zhongchen Tomato Products Co., Ltd. (hereinafter referred to as "Tianjin Zhongchen"), another holding company of Chalkis, to pave the way for financial fraud in the following years. In 2007, Liu Yi, chairman of Chalkis, invited Wu Xin'an, former head of the sales department of Chalkis and current independent businessman, to participate in Chalkis's financial fraud. After Wu Xin'an joined, Xinjiang Haoke International Trade Co., Ltd. (hereinafter referred to as "Xinjiang Haoke") under his control purchased tomato ketchup from Tianjin Shengzhong and sold it to Tianjin Zhongcheng after gaining profits from certain price markups. After completing the product transaction in the entire sales chain, Chalkis only changed the location for product storage, but in nature, it relocated its own stock from left hand to right hand, and ultimately achieved the purpose of false increases in the revenue and profits of the main business.

Financial Fraud Case of Xintai Electric

Dandong Xintai Electric Co., Ltd. (stock code: 300372) was changed from Dandong Rectifier Co., Ltd. on July 25, 2007, with registered capital of 70 million Yuan. It is among the first batch of newly recognized high-tech enterprises in Liaoning Province and one of the key high-tech enterprises under the China Torch Program. On January 27, 2014, Xintai Electric was listed on the Growth Enterprises Market of the Shenzhen Stock Exchange. In the annual on-the-spot inspection by Liaoning Supervisory Bureau of China Securities Regulatory Commission in May 2015, Xintai Electric was found to have problems in untruthful financial data. After four months of investigation, the following conclusions were drawn. Firstly, there was false financial data recorded in the IPO application documents. Secondly, false records and major omissions were found in the periodical statements disclosed after listing. Finally, the intermediary failed to perform its due diligence. As of July 2016, Xintai Electric was ordered to correct, warned and fined 8,320,000 Yuan, and Wen Deyi, the actual controller, was warned and fined 8,920,000 Yuan, the chief accountant was warned and fined 600,000 Yuan, and other persons concerned were punished accordingly. On August 26, 2016, according to Provisions on the Transfer of Suspectable Criminal Cases by Administrative Organs for Law Enforcement, China Securities Regulatory Commission decided to transfer Xintai Electric and related personnel suspected of fraudulent issuance and other related crimes to the public security organization and to investigate criminal responsibility according to law, after a special consultation with the public security organization.

Chapter Summary

This chapter reviews the different perspectives of prospect theory and financial fraud and their evolution. From the perspective of prospect theory, there are different viewpoints in the academic circles on the relationship between external governance mechanisms and corporate violations. The positive side believes that external expectations are beneficial to enhance the achievement motives of agents, thereby reducing the possibility of enterprises to engage in any behavior against regulations, while the negative side believes that external governance will reduce the managerial autonomy of the actors and propel them to rationalize their violations, so that it will be more likely for the enterprises to go against regulations. This book holds that the main problem that causes the logical contradiction is that there are certain regulatory factors between external governance mechanisms and corporate violations.

As an important basis for external stakeholders to make governance decisions, performance plays an important role in the strategic choice of enterprises in the operating process. Therefore, the relationship between performance pressure and financial fraud is of great theoretical value as the basic framework of prospect theory analysis. What's more, through in-depth analysis of the relevant research on financial fraud, the author has found that the perspective of prospect theory has integrated the great achievements made by the past scholars, and is the closest to the real situation. From the perspective of prospect theory, financial fraud research attaches increasing importance to the inhibitory effect of external governance mechanism on financial fraud. For this reason, this book chooses performance pressure as the main antecedent to explore the psychological mechanism of senior executives engaged in financial fraud. According to prospect theory, all decisions are a balancing process between costs and benefits, which means that the cost-benefit balance between CEO and senior executives plays a crucial rule in this process.

Generally speaking, the external governance mechanism, internal governance mechanism and the psychological characteristics of senior executives are the main areas of financial fraud analysis in the existing literature. However, the existing literature has not yet analyzed financial fraud from the perspective integration of these three perspectives. To make up for the deficiency, In order to remedy this deficiency, this book, based on performance feedback, regresses the institution-related elements, such as financing demand, institutional efficiency, political connection of senior executives and enterprise property rights, and then explores the cost-benefit balance mechanism of financial fraud under performance pressure from the perspective of motive, opportunity and rationalization.

Chapter 3 Theoretical Analysis and Research Hypotheses

This chapter determines the theoretical basis of this study based on the aforementioned literature review, and constructs the research model and hypothesis on the basis of the existing theories.

Performance Pressure and Financial Fraud

Capital markets have been supposed for a long time to exert tremendous pressure on enterprises to ensure the achievement of short-term business objectives, resulting in managers' short-sighted acts, such as focusing more on the achievement of current performance at the expense of long-term development (Bhojraj & Libby, 2005; Bushee, 1998; Laverty, 1996; Marginson & Mcaulay, 2008; Porter, 1992; Stein, 1989). For managers, one of the most important sources of pressure is performance pressure of the enterprise. According to the classic principal-agent theory, the performance evaluation of enterprises has become an important indicator to measure managers' managerial capacity and performance due to the separation of ownership and management power in enterprises (Zhang & Gimeno, 2010). As far as managers are concerned, the enterprise itself will set an expected goal for future performance according to the historical records, but when its performance is lower than expected goal, it will exert strong market pressure on the organization and its managers (Zhang & Gimeno, 2010), which will cause the management to be censured by shareholders, thus going ill with the evaluation of the management at the end of the year and affecting their salary, welfare, reputation and even career development. Narayanan (1985) found that once the company's performance published regularly fails to meet market expectations, it will make the investors less willing to invest in the company, resulting in a decline in the company's market value and an increase in the probability that managers will be replaced. Such performance pressure may affect the follow-up decision-making behavior of organizations and their managers (Hayes & Levine, 2000), and pose a significant impact on corporate decision-making of strategies and investments (Jensen, 2005; Porter, 1992; Stein, 1989).

Pursuant to the viewpoints of the strategic choice school, when the company's actual performance is lower than its expected performance, it will affect risk-taking (Bromiley, 1991; Deephouse & Wiseman, 2000; Fiegenbaum & Thomas, 1988; Gooding et al., 1996), investments in corporate R & D (Bromiley & Washburn, 2011; Chen & Miller, 2007), capital structure (Miller & Bromiley, 1990), actual and expected enterprise growth (Greve, 2008; Wicklund & Shepherd, 2003), large-scale organizational change (Greve, 1998), alliance choice (Baum et al., 2005), innovation (Greve, 2003a), diversification (Palmer & Wiseman, 1999), capital investment (Greve, 2003b), business unit stripping (Shimizu, 2007), security operations (Baum & Dahlin, 2007), mergers and acquisitions (Iyer & Miller, 2008) and organizational misconduct (Harris & Bromiley, 2007). In consideration of the impact of performance feedbacks and performance prospects on enterprises' search behavior, Chen (2008) found that the problem-driven search activities would be intensified when the company perceived that it was difficult to meet their performance target for the next year.

According to the performance feedback theory, performance expectation is an important reference point for enterprises to make strategic decisions. Organizational change is most likely to occur when performance is lower than, rather than higher than, the expected level. But when performance is higher than the expected level, firms may tend to maintain the status quo (Bromiley, Miller & Rau, 2001), avoid those acts that may lead to performance decline (March & Shapira, 1987), and pursue higher performance (Cyert & March, 1963). However, when the performance is lower than the expected level, managers tend to take proactive risk-taking strategies to alleviate the pressure of the company, and improve the performance of the company by means of financial fraud.

On the one hand, when the company's performance is lower than the expected level, it will threaten the legitimacy of the survival of the company, and the reasons for the existence of the organization will be questioned by stakeholders, which will bring huge losses to the interests of the organization and its managers. Once the firm's actual performance falls below the expected level, the unexpected negative earnings which are not predicted by investors and analysts will be magnified, and as the external pressures on the firm increase, analysts and markets will take over-reaction towards such unexpected earnings performance (Bondt & Thaler, 1985),, which will result in a downgrade of the firm (Wiersema & Zhang, 2011), a decline in stock price (Kasznik & McNichols, 2002; Bartov et al., 2002; Mishina et al., 2010), and a decline in its market value (Bartov et al., 2002). Moreover, it will further arouse the close attention of investors, substantial shareholders and the board of directors, increase the risk of managers' positions (Wiersema & Zhang, 2011), lower their wages (Matsunaga & Park, 2001), and even make them leave office (Hall & Liebman, 1998), which will cause great market pressure on managers (Gentry & Shen, 2013). Furthermore, it will have a significant impact on managers' professional and private wealth, as well as urge the organization and self-interested managers to strive to achieve or surpass the existing gap in performance expectations (Bartov et al., 2002; Burgstahler & Dichev, 1997; Puffer & Weintrop, 1991; Gentry & Shen, 2013).

On the other hand, managers are not always short-sighted and egoistic (Amihud & Lev, 1981; Jensen & Meckling, 1976), and they will be more inclined to take risks when the actual performance of the enterprise is lower than the expected level (Cyert & March, 1963). Prospect theory (Kahneman & Tversky, 1979) holds that the decision makers of bounded rationality tend to decide the follow-up behavior decisions based on the gap between the actual performance and the expected level. In case that the actual performance is lower than the expected level, the decision maker will define such state below expectation as a state of loss. When the actual performance is higher than the expected level, the decision maker will define the state above expectation as a state of gain (March & Simon, 1958). The state of loss promotes managers to try exploratory risk-taking behavior to achieve the expected level of organizational performance (Cyert & March, 1963). Based on the logic of this theory, enterprises will choose to take risks to improve the level of short-term real earnings under the pressure of external capital markets, in case that the real earnings of enterprises are lower than the expected level of earnings predicted by external analysts. However, the risk-taking decision-making behavior of enterprises is not only reflected in the positive creative production activities, but the innovation of entrepreneurs does not necessarily contribute to the society, the root for which is that they fail to take into account the impact of their activities on the society in the process of pursuing innovation, or even the systematic destruction of the Veblen style may occur (Veblen,1904). The entrepreneur theory of Baumol (1990, 1993) has made it clear that entrepreneurs' intelligence can be allocated among various uses, and that the supply of entrepreneurship activities is unbalanced among all social strata, among which there not only efficient production activities, such as technological change and innovation, but also unproductive activities, such as rent-seeking, as well as destructive entrepreneurship activities, such as crime, illegal business and so forth. Furthermore, destructive production activities, like violations, are very common in the business circles. It is estimated that 10% of GNP is used for rent-seeking and other unproductive activities (Baumol, 1990). After 30 years of development, private enterprises in China have made brilliant achievements, and their innovative ability and transformative ability have been gradually enhanced. On the other hand, the negative news about tax evasion, environmental pollution, embezzlement of wages, and bribery by private enterprises in China has never ceased. Tunneling by substantial shareholders, related party transactions and other moral hazards have been often seen in capital markets. Some scholars estimate that rent-seeking and corruption may account for 20% to 30% of GDP in China (Sheng, 2012).

Based on this, we believe that when the company's actual performance is lower than expected performance, managers may eliminate such performance pressure through a variety of financial fraud methods, such as fictitious accounting information, profit manipulation or earnings management. This approach can raise the actual earnings in a quick, effective and low-cost way, thus alleviating the performance pressure on managers (Kasznik & McNichols, 2002), especially avoiding their potential career risks (Puffer & Weintrop, 1991) and the losses of personal wealth (Gentry & Shen, 2013). In consideration of other positive and creative risk-taking decision-making behaviors, they play a role in enhancing the long-term performance of enterprises, such as increasing capital investments and enhancing marketing promotion or R&D investments, but these investments have long return cycles, high risks and high uncertainty, especially no effectiveness in the short term (Pindyck, 1982; Zaheer et al., 1999; March, 1991). It is really difficult to have a positive and immediate impact on the company's real earnings

(Scherer & Ross, 1990; Porter, 1992; Jensen, 2005; Mizik, 2010). Even due to the increase in various investment costs of the company, its current real earnings may seem to be much worse (Gentry & Shen, 2013). Baumgartner et al. (2009) and Oliver & Holzinger (2008) also found that, compared with aggressive strategies such as strategic change and innovation input, enterprises with poor performance are more likely to choose defensive strategies like financial fraud, the root cause for which is that the enterprises with poor operating performance have more serious internal structure contradiction with lower organizational efficiency and greater difficulties in coordination (Bombardini, 2008). In this case, the adoption of aggressive strategies in enterprises can not improve the business performance of enterprises, but may further aggravate the decline of business performance.

Therefore, in the case of performance pressures, it has become a strategic choice for managers to extricate themselves from performance dilemma and improve short-term performance under pressure by taking risk-taking and speculations with little investment but quick result and raising the actual earnings in a low-cost, quick and effective manner by means of financial misrepresentation or profit falsification. Based on this, we propose the following hypotheses:

H1: With the increase of enterprises' historical performance pressures, enterprises will adopt higher illegal financial frauds.

H2: With the increase of enterprises' industry performance pressures, enterprises will adopt higher illegal financial frauds.

Adjustment of Corporate Political Connection

Based on the above analysis, historical performance pressures and industry performance pressures of enterprises are important motives for enterprises to choose financial fraud. With the continuous improvement of historical performance and industry performance pressures, enterprises are more likely to choose financial fraud. However, it is believed in this study that the behavioral decision-making of an enterprise is closely bound up with its internal and external environmental factors. Financial fraud is a type of violation. Enterprise managers are faced with the balance between benefit and cost when making this decision, and the internal and external environment that enterprises are faced with is an important factor determining their benefits and costs. Thus, in this study, the author examines the three influencing factors at the organizational, industrial and regional levels based on the unique institutional environment and the characteristics of organizational resources in China during the transition period. Firstly, the author mainly discusses the influence of political connection and enterprises' financing demand.

The phenomenon of enterprises establishing political connection is commonly seen all over the world, especially in developing countries with relatively backward systems (Faccio, 2006; Yu & Pan, 2008; Wu et al., 2009; Liu et al., 2010). Entrepreneurs often engage in activities organized by political parties or government departments to establish contacts with government officials for the purpose of obtaining political asylum or economic benefits (Zhang & Zhang, 2005). In the process of China's economic transformation, the decentralization reform between the central and local governments and the GDP-based competition among the governments induce local governments to pay more attention to economic development. Once local governments are given the priority to manage local social and economic affairs, it has naturally become one of the important strategies of various enterprises to establish relations with the governments (Yang, 2011). Political constraints are indeed a necessary condition for entrepreneurship and business growth (Aldrich & Wiedenmayer, 1993; Bird, 1989). Zhou Xiaohu (2006) summarized the impact of social networks on international entrepreneurship, including the creation of new international business opportunities, such as access to new markets through customer relations, acquisition of information and knowledge needed for enterprise internationalization and timely access to market information necessary for decision-making, in order to accelerate the pace of international expansion for enterprises.

Pan Hongbo et al. (2008) studied the performance changes of listed companies with government background before and after acquisition of non-listed companies, and found that political connection can guarantee the relative independence of enterprise property rights from local governments. Political connection not only affects corporate behavior by influencing the formulation of government policies at the macro level, but also affects corporate value by influencing corporate financing behavior, business behavior and ownership structure at the micro level. For instance, political connection can influence capital allocation by influencing government policy or the allocation mechanisms of financial aids, and enhance the value of enterprises. In emerging capital markets such as Indonesia, political connection can increase the probability that the enterprises obtain debt financing, enjoy lower tax rates and higher market shares (Faccio, 2004; Leuz & Flex, 2005). Political connection influences corporate governance and then corporate value through the ownership structure, which is not only manifested in the impact on internal governance mechanism, but also directly manifested in the impact on external governance mechanism. On the other hand, the negative effects of political connection on enterprises can not be neglected (Fan et al., 2007; Qian et al., 2011; He et al., 2013). To be concrete, political connection aggravates the predatory behavior of controlling shareholders, especially when the rights and interests of investors are protected at a low level (Pan & Yu, 2008). The political connection of senior executives has effectively consolidated their position, while corporate governance is greatly constrained in the process of supervision and restraint. Moreover, for the sake of private interests, the economic behavior of senior executives is likely to deviate from the goal of maximizing shareholders' interests, and the political relations they establish are also mainly for their own benefits (You et al., 2010).

From the perspective of the social capital theory, Wu Jingfei and He Dajun et al. (2008) studied 210 listed companies in Shanghai Stock Exchange, and carried out an empirical study on the relationship between political networking of senior managers and diversification strategy of these companies based on the analysis of panel data for three consecutive years from 2004 to 2006. The author distinguishes the connotation and measurement of social capital. It is necessary to explain the level and perspective of analysis based on the theory, since the connotation and operational measurement of the concept of social capital may vary from each other because of the research questions and the choice of analysis level and perspective. This study abandons functionalism and accepts structuralism as its theoretical basis, defining social capital as the structure of social networks embedded in individuals (or groups, organizations). Entrepreneur's political relation network is defined as the relationship between the enterprise and the government, one of the most important stakeholders for the enterprise, also known as the political networking or political connection of senior executives in the enterprise. It is also pointed out that most previous studies have focused on the impact of top managers' or directors' private political relationships on the performance or value of the enterprises, while less attention has been paid to the relationship between top managers' private political relations and strategic behavior of enterprises. Zhou Xiaohu (2006) summarized the impact of social networks on international entrepreneurship, including the creation of new international business opportunities, such as access to new markets through customer relations, acquisition of information and knowledge needed for enterprise internationalization and timely access to market information necessary for decision-making, which can accelerate the speed of international expansion of the enterprises. Pan Hongbo, Xia Xinping and Yu Minggui (2008) studied the changes of market performance of listed companies before and after mergers and acquisitions in the context of the acquisition of non-listed companies by listed companies that are controlled by local governments, and found that the political connection of enterprises can protect their property rights from damage by local governments.

Betrand et al. (2004) believed that in France, the CEO of a company, who graduated from an elite school, used to serve in a government department or was currently a senior official, was deemed to have political relations. Chen Donghua (2003), Fan et al. (2007) depicted the government background to examine the proportion of directors with government background among board members. This book describes the political relations of private enterprises by finding out the information of the directors of the board, and then figuring out whether he or she is a member of the National People's Congress, a member of the CPPCC or a former member of the government department according to his or her personal information, which will help to depict the political relations of private listed companies in an all-round way. The political relationship of private listed companies is measured by the ratio of directors with political background in the board (PC rate).

Lei Guangyong, Li Shufeng and Wang Xiujuan (2009) pointed out that the influence of political connection on corporate value is mainly achieved through the helping hand or the grabbing hand of government intervention by direct and indirect means, among which the former includes political connection that enables enterprises to obtain preferential bank loans, tax incentives, policy subsidies, stock issuance rights and franchise rights, and the latter includes political connection that influences the operation of corporate governance mechanism through the arrangement of ownership nature and ownership structure. Among them, the employment of high-quality external audits is one of the important manifestations of an effective corporate governance structure. The influence path of political connection on corporate performance and value is affected not only by internal factors, such as company background, financial leverage and ownership nature or structure (Faccio, 2004; Li, Meng & Zhang, 2006), but also by external factors, such as market environment, especially legal environment (Morck, Wolfenzon & Yeung, 2005). In the emerging capital market, the government's acts tend to be less standardized and less restrained by the law, but government intervention has a great impact on economic activities (Leuz & Flex, 2005).

Political connection not only affects corporate behavior by influencing the formulation of government policies at the macro level, but also affects corporate value by influencing corporate financing behavior, business behavior and ownership structure at the micro level. For instance, political connection can influence capital allocation by influencing government policy or the allocation mechanisms of financial aids, and enhance the value of enterprises. In emerging capital markets such as Indonesia, political connection can increase the probability that the enterprises obtain debt financing, enjoy lower tax rates and higher market shares (Faccio, 2004; Leuz & Flex, 2005). Political connection influences corporate governance and then corporate value through the ownership structure, which is not only manifested in the impact on internal governance mechanism, but also directly manifested in the impact on external governance mechanism.

External audit, especially high-quality external audit, is one of the most important external governance mechanisms of a company, and its impact on corporate value can be achieved mainly by means of the reduction of information asymmetry, effective supervision of insiders, and signal transmission and compensation guarantee (Menon & Williams, 1994; Baber, Kumar & Verghese, 1995). The role of external audit in corporate governance is influenced by external environment, especially legal environment. Studies have shown that as long as the legal system provides effective incentives and constraints to a certain extent, high-quality external audits can still be realized, and that even in countries with poor legal environment, external audits can still play a part in external corporate governance, as well as replace the legal institutional arrangements that provide less protection for the rights and interests of investors (Choi & Wong, 2005). The author points out that the various regions in China develop their economics at an unbalanced rate, and have a huge gap in the rule of law, so that political connection can be more deeply involved in the specific business activities of enterprises, which will pose a profound impact on the differences in the needs and choices of external audit.

Wu Wenfeng, Wu Chongfeng and Rui Meng (2009) defined the government background of senior executives in enterprises as a form of corporate political connection (political connection/ political-connection/ political relationship) mentioned in foreign literature. Political connection refers to the implicit political relationship between a company and an individual with political power. In foreign countries, the interest relationship between the company and government officials or members of the Congress in the form of election fund-raising is deemed as a political connection. In China, senior executives in a company who used to serve as government officials are considered to have a government background as well as a political connection. Taking private enterprises listed in the Shanghai and Shenzhen stock exchanges from 1999 to 2004 as samples, the author conducted an empirical analysis of the impact of the experience of corporate senior executives as a member of central or local governments on the acquisition of tax incentives for enterprises. The results showed that, in provinces and cities where enterprises have a heavy burden beyond tax, the applicable tax rate and actual rate of income tax of the companies where the senior executives have government background are significantly lower than those of the companies where the senior executives do not have government background, and that the higher the heavier the extra-tax burden of enterprises in the province and city where the company is located, the more tax incentives the senior executives with government background will obtain.

As for bank loans, it is consistent with the conclusions of the existing literature. However, the more loans an enterprise with political connection receives, the easier it will be to overinvest, which will have a negative impact on the value of the enterprise. For this reason, political connection has a significant negative impact on the allocation efficiency of credit resources, which will lead to deviation in the allocation of credit resources. Chen Shuangying, Jing Runtian et al. (2010) pointed out that the social capital of private entrepreneurs is a positive response to the failure of market and government laws, and that the relationship network, the essential feature of social relationship capital, formed valuable resources in innovation activities, and provided collectively owned capital for members of the network. Social relationship capital mainly comes from the membership of special networks in the form of social status or reputation, which is embedded in mutual recognition or widely acknowledged networks. Based on such networking connection, members in the network will have an access to various kinds of innovation resources and be able to identify different innovation opportunities. This book divides the social capital of private entrepreneurs into banking relationship capital, association relationship capital and political relationship capital, and studies the impact of social relationship capital of private entrepreneurs on the decisions in R&D investments, and conducts an empirical study based on the data. The results show that banking relationship capital and association relationship capital of private enterprises will promote the tendency and intensity of R&D investment, while political relationship capital may hinder the tendency and intensity of R&D investment.

Based on the summary of the existing research on political connection, it was found that there were two main types of impacts of political connection on enterprises:

On the one hand, political connection is conducive to promoting the performance of enterprises, such as helping enterprises to improve access to loans, preferential tax rates, and the possibility of higher market share (Faccio, 2006). When faced with problems, companies with political connections are more likely to be supported by the government to tide them over (Faccio et al., 2006).

On the other hand, political connection may have a significant impact on the economic consequences of enterprises, which is reflected in various aspects. First of all, political connection may boost the value of enterprises (Faccio, 2006). However, it argues in more books that political connection will result in negative economic consequences. Chaney et al. (2007) found that the quality of accounting information of the enterprises with political connection is significantly lower than that of the enterprises without political connection. Chen et al. (2007) found that analysts' prediction errors for companies with political connections were significantly greater than those for the enterprises without political connection. Faccio et al. (2006) found that although the enterprises with political connection are more likely to get support from the government when they are in a pickle, their performance after getting support is still significantly weaker than that of the enterprises without political connection. Fan et al. (2007) argued that after the IPO, the performance of the enterprises with political connection declined significantly less than that of the enterprises without political connection.

The reason why political connection leads to negative speculative or opportunistic behavior is that these actions can help to gain benefits directly and quickly, thus compensating for the cost of constructing political connection (Morck et al., 2004). In particular, when the enterprise is in a relatively difficult business situation, the strategy that depends on political connection to engage in positive and long-term investments fails to reverse the plight of the enterprise in a short time. On the contrary, in this case, they are more likely to rely on the asylum role of political relations to engage in the investment projects with little investment but quick result, or even destructive acts violating laws and rules (He et al., 2013). Moreover, the existence of political connection enhances the institutional autonomy of these enterprises (Lian et al., 2015), especially allowing these enterprises to be seldom subject to political constraints of government departments, so that they will have increasing space to engage in destructive production activities accordingly (Berkman et al., 2011). More importantly, political connection can affect the efficiency of law enforcement of investors and lower the effectiveness of market regulation (Xu et al., 2013). Even if the actors who own political connection violate the rules and laws, political connection will become their umbrella to shelter managers or enterprises from sanctions imposed by those in power (Anderson, 2000; Qian et al., 2011; Xu et al., 2013), which is because listed companies with government background engaged in violations usually take advantage of political resources to obstruct and delay the investigation of regulators, so as to reduce the timeliness of the investigation and punishment of violations (Xu et al., 2013).

Xu Nianhang et al. (2013) found that the senior executives of the enterprises with political connection are far less likely to be punished for violations than the enterprises without political connection. Even if the company is punished for violations, its punishment is difficult to be effectively implemented as long as its senior executives are closely linked with government departments (Anderson, 2000). Sun et al. (2006) further found that senior executives of companies that violate the rules are more likely to leave office, but there are still a lot of opportunities for them to work in other companies or even be promoted after leaving. The senior executive concerned who is a Party member is likely to be punished less severely. In case that the defendant is a person concerned with political connections, it is often impossible for law enforcement departments to remain neutral and impartial (La Porta et al., 2004). Based on the asylum effect of the umbrella of political connection, this book argues that enterprises with political connection are more likely to engage in financial fraud under performance pressure, in consideration of the comparison between cost and benefit. In this way, on the one hand, it can change the backward operating performance of the enterprise in a short time. On the other hand, due to the asylum effect of political connection, managers will not worry about worry about being punished and punished by government departments and paying too high a price. Especially with the increasing pressure of business operation, managers will be much more motivated accordingly to turn around the predicament through financial fraud.

H3: With the increase of historical performance pressure, enterprises with the background of government relations are more likely to engage in illegal financial fraud.

H4: With the increase of industry performance pressure, enterprises with the background of government relations are more likely to engage in illegal financial fraud.

Adjustment of Financing Demand

Generally speaking, it is difficult for an enterprise to meet all the capital requirements for its operation only with its own funds. As an important practical problem enterprises are faced with, financing has been widely concerned in the field of financial research (Lu & Zhang, 2014). In recent years, the Chinese government has made great efforts to boost the construction of capital market, and adopted a number of measures, such as the construction of stock and bond markets, the commercial management of state-owned banks, and the relaxation of private capital into the financial industry, but the financing bottleneck of Chinese enterprises has not been really overcome (Xu & Zhou, 2016).

Modigliani & Miller (1958) believed that under ideal conditions, capital should be freely circulated, and enterprises can obtain capital pursuant to their own needs. Therefore, the internal and external capital markets can be completely replaced in theory. But in practice, the ideal state does not exist. Because of information asymmetry and transaction costs arising in the capital market, there are differences in capital cost between internal and external capital markets, and the cost of the acquisition of external capital is higher than that of internal capital, thus developing certain financing constraints. The higher the degree of financing constraints is, the higher the financing costs paid by enterprises will be and the less willing the enterprises will be to finance. Therefore, according to the principle of pecking order, enterprises give priority to the use of their own funds, followed by debt financing, and finally equity financing.

In terms of internal funds, enterprises maintain their operations based on their own funds, which has the advantage of low cost, but there are also two deficiencies. On the one hand, it takes an enterprise a longer time to accumulate its own funds, which will be not conducive to business expansion and opportunity grasp of the enterprise (Pollet & Wilson, 2008). On the other hand, the company's own funds will be affected by the supply of funds at the upstream and downstream of the supply chain, and thus it is not necessarily able to arrive on time. In this regard, overdependence on its own funds will lead to the risk of capital chain rupture.

In terms of debt financing, since the bank and other creditors decide the scale, duration and interest rate of the loan according to the financial condition of the debtor, the debtor may be motivated to engage in financial fraud in order to gain a vantage ground in the negotiation on the debt contract, and the more the company deviates from the terms of the debt contract, the more likely the company will be to commit financial fraud (Franz et al., 2014). Valipour & Moradbeygi (2011) found that in order to enhance the bargaining power in debt negotiations, the enterprise with financing demand will deliver its earnings information the bank, and that the higher the financing demand is, the more likely the company will be to engage in financial fraud. Rao Yanchao and Hu Yiming (2005) found that banks mainly take financial statements as the basis for arranging loan issuance, in which profit is an extremely important reference index, thus forming the incentive for debtors to whitewash their financial surplus.

In terms of equity financing, China's stock market is strictly controlled by the government, while the company's IPO, issuance of additional shares and other equity financing methods need to be examined and approved by government departments at all levels. Especially, there are high requirements for the performance of enterprises, such as continuous profits in the past three years, no more than 50% decrease in operating profit in the year of stock issuance compared with the previous year and standard auditing report issued. In order to raise the issue price of stock and reduce the financing cost, the company will be strongly motivated to commit financial fraud in order to achieve IPO and rigid conditions for additional issuance and maximize its own interests (Cai et al., 2013).

In a word, when the performance of listed companies fails to meet the analyst's expectations, it will lead to a decline in the market value of the company and a fall in its stock price, a decrease in the size of the company's capital from the capital market, but also increase the cost of equity financing, and even result in the rupture of the company's capital chain. Watts (2003) believes that capital market motive is one of the motives for earnings management, and that senior executives of enterprises have a driving force for earnings management in order to carry out IPO and SEO. Teoh et al. (1998) also found that senior executives of enterprises facing financing constraints are more likely to change their financial activities, such as manipulating earnings, in order to achieve the corresponding earnings targets to achieve the corresponding earnings objectives to get rid of financing difficulties and increase the availability of external financing. Liao Xiumei (2007) found that the bank's earnings management of senior executives can be identified, and that banks may increase the interest rate of loans to lower their own risks and related losses, in order to ensure that their legitimate rights and interests are not damaged. As an important channel for enterprises to have access to funds, banks and other financial institutions are inseparable from the financing activities of enterprises. A vast majority of creditors pay attention to the business performance of enterprises when offering a loan, while the enterprises with poor business performance may be bound by more restrictive loan terms, which tend to associate their financing activities with financial fraud.

Li Zengfu et al. (2013) also found that the company has engaged in financial frauds in the research on the private placement of equity. In terms of debt financing, since the bank and other creditors decide the scale, duration and interest rate of the loan according to the financial condition of the debtor, the debtor may be motivated to engage in financial fraud in order to gain a vantage ground in the negotiation on the debt contract, and the more the company deviates from the terms of the debt contract, the more likely the company will be to commit financial fraud (Franz et al., 2014). Valipour & Moradbeygi (2011) found that in order to enhance the bargaining power in debt negotiations, the enterprise with financing demand will deliver its earnings information the bank, and that the higher the financing demand is, the more likely the company will be to engage in financial fraud. Rao Yanchao and Hu Yiming (2005) found that banks mainly take financial statements as the basis for arranging loan issuance, in which profit is an extremely important reference index, thus forming the incentive for debtors to whitewash their financial surplus.

Previous studies have found that when the company's performance is lower than the expected level, potential investors and other stakeholders will not support the company in a pickle, which will aggravate the risk of the company going bankrupt. Therefore, when the company has demand for debt financing, it will be motivated to engage in financial fraud. As far as managers are concerned, when the company has greater financing demand, the lower the actual performance of the company is than the expected level, the greater the performance pressure on managers will be. Managers will be forced to engage in financial fraud in order to avoid the loss of personal income and the rupture of the company's capital chain caused by the failure of actual performance to meet the expected level. On this basis, this book proposes the following hypotheses:

H5: The higher the financing demand of the company is, the greater illegal financial fraud the company will engage in with the increase in its historical performance pressure.

H6: The higher the financing demand of the company is, the greater illegal financial fraud the company will engage in with the increase in its industry performance pressure.

Adjustment of Industry Competition

Industry competition, as an important index to measure the distribution of resources within the industry, plays a decisive role in enterprises' strategic decision-making (Li & Zhang, 2010). In the SCP (Structure – Conduct - Performance) model, the classical analysis framework of the Harvard School in the theory of industrial organization, the degree of industry competition, as the main component of market structure, is of vital significance to enterprises' strategic decision-making. In the framework of SCP analysis, market competition is divided into two levels, perfect competition and monopoly, while the real market is analyzed as a case between the two extreme situations, where the analysis logic holds that the number of enterprises in the market, as a criterion for improving relative efficiency, directly determines the efficiency of resource allocation in the market. When there are a larger number of enterprises in the market, the industry is in a perfectly competitive state, which can effectively improve the allocation efficiency of market resources, while the decision makers in enterprises may tend to make risky decisions. When there are a smaller number of enterprises in the market, the industry is in an oligopoly state in the Cournot competition model, where the enterprise has a high market return but market resources are allocated in a less effective way, and then the enterprise tends to make conservative decisions (Fang, 2011; Lai, 2012).

How will the degree of industry competition affect managers' decision-making? Previous studies have found that when the industry is in a highly competitive state, there will be more prominent motives for the enterprises to take certain offensive or defensive actions in competition in order to gain or maintain competitive advantage, but the depth and breadth of the impact are less restricted by the reaction of other competitors in the industry. In this case, enterprises are more constrained by each other but less dependent on each other, and the predatory effect shows fast frequency and low degree and other characteristics with little investment but quick result. However, when the industry is in a poorly competitive state and the market is less uncertain, it will be more accurate for enterprises to conduct scenario analysis. There is a decline in the frequency of the enterprise making decisions on offensive and defensive competitive behavior, but it has much more definite goals, and the decision has a greater impact on the enterprise, in which the enterprise may either amaze the world with a single brilliant feat or loss the whole game with one careless act, so that the predatory effect of enterprises presents the characteristics of low frequency but deep degree (Chen & Wang, 2013).

For managers, the more fierce the market competition is, the greater the performance pressure they will face when the actual performance is lower than the expected level. On the one hand, in the context of fierce industry competition, the signal released by the decline of performance pressures of enterprises is more likely to make enterprises in a tight spot, which leads to enterprises being easily abandoned by their stakeholders. In a perfectly competitive industry, the allocation of resources mainly depends on market-oriented allocation, and the performance of enterprises directly reflects their real competitive power. When the actual performance is lower than the performance expectation, the direct signal released is the weakening of the competitiveness of enterprises, which will cause the stakeholders to question the managerial capacity of the enterprises (Zhong & Fan, 2004). In the meantime, over-publicity of the performance decline of an enterprise by its competitors may also lead to the loss of the enterprise's reputation in the market (Lian et al., 2014). Based on the study on the data of enterprises in developing countries, Laurence (2001) found that the more competitive the industry is, the more intensely the managers will conduct earnings management. As far as managers are concerned, when the industry competition becomes more intense, the performance decline of an enterprise may directly lead the enterprise to get into business distress or even go bankrupt. In order to avoid personal loss of managers and reputation loss in the job market, enterprises will have stronger motives for financial fraud.

On the other hand, Istaitieh & Rodriguez (2003) collected a large amount of financial data of Spanish manufacturing enterprises in order to study the relationship between capital structure decision-making and product market competition of enterprises, and carried out regression analysis with the panel data. The results showed that industries with stronger product market competition tend to choose more risky capital decisions, which mean the choice of a higher debt level, while the industries with weaker product market competition tend to choose more conservative financial strategies. Fosu (2013) collected financial data of 257 enterprises in South Africa from 1998 to 2009 for panel data analysis, and found that the degree of industry competition enables the enterprise to play a more prominent role as financial leverage, and then increase their debts. For managers, the decline in the actual performance of enterprises will directly lead to the enterprises put in a tight spot. In this case, they are more likely to adopt risk-taking strategies for financial fraud. On this basis, this book proposes the following hypotheses:

H7: The fiercer the competition in the industry where the company is located is, the greater illegal financial fraud the company will engage in with the increase in its historical performance pressure.

H8: The fiercer the competition in the industry where the company is located is, the greater illegal financial fraud the company will engage in with the increase in its industry performance pressure.

Adjustment of Institutional Environment

Institution, a consensus norm formulated by human beings to restrict human interaction, is the foundation for human exchange. The exchange here includes political, economic and social exchange behavior (North, 1990). Douglass C. North made a penetrating analysis of the importance of institutional environment in the book Institutions, Institutional Change and Economic Performance. Government and market are two main ways of resource allocation. The view of free market theory holds that the adequate market competition mechanism provides information and incentives for individual decision makers, and can achieve the effective allocation of resources to the maximum extent. Welfare economics also holds that if Walras equilibrium exists in a competitive market, the equilibrium must reach Pareto optimum, and that the resource allocation model in market competition is optimal, while the government just needs to play the role of night watcher (Smith, 1776). However, in compliance with the hypothesis of rational man, there are some inevitable problems in the freely competitive market, such as monopoly, externality and information asymmetry, which eventually lead to market failure.

Government and market are two main ways of resource allocation. The view of free market theory holds that the adequate market competition mechanism provides information and incentives for individual decision makers, and can achieve the effective allocation of resources to the maximum extent. Welfare economics also holds that if Walras equilibrium exists in a competitive market, the equilibrium must reach Pareto optimum, and that the resource allocation model in market competition is optimal, while the government just needs to play the role of night watcher (Smith, 1776). However, in compliance with the hypothesis of rational man, there are some inevitable problems in the freely competitive market, such as monopoly, externality and information asymmetry, which eventually lead to market failure. How to effectively avoid market failure provides the main theoretical basis for government regulation. The public interest theory represented by Arthur Cecil Pigou (2007) holds that government regulation can effectively avoid market failure, optimize the allocation of market resources and improve public welfare in society (Musgrave, 1959; ATkinson & Stiglitz, 1980).

However, in the meantime, the view of the public choice school holds that government intervention is not always effective. On the one hand, the government may also face the problem of public failure. On the other hand, the motives of government intervention in the market are often questioned, as the government is more likely to create rent and seek political purposes, rather than simply to maximize social welfare (Buchanan & Tullock, 1962; Olson, 1965). Stigler (1971) even pointed out that the government's control tends to be captured by the existing enterprises in the market, which seek strict control policies by bribing or transferring rents to prevent and restrict the entry of potential enterprises into the market, in order to maintain their monopoly status and high monopoly rents in the market. It is ubiquitous for the government to allocate resources in various countries, where the only difference is the power and coverage of resource allocation, while the formal institution tends to be regarded as an important basis for rigorous restriction and constraint of resource allocation of the government (Klapper et al., 2009). The existing analysis of formal institution and entrepreneurship activities mainly examines the restriction of formal institution on resource allocation of the government to affect entrepreneurship.

How to effectively avoid market failure provides the main theoretical basis for government regulation. The public interest theory represented by Arthur Cecil Pigou (2007) holds that government regulation can effectively avoid market failure, optimize the allocation of market resources and improve public welfare in society (Musgrave, 1959; ATkinson & Stiglitz, 1980). However, in the meantime, the view of the public choice school holds that government intervention is not always effective. On the one hand, the government may also face the problem of public failure. On the other hand, the motives of government intervention in the market are often questioned, as the government is more likely to create rent and seek political purposes, rather than simply to maximize social welfare. (Buchanan & Tullock, 1962; Olson, 1965). Stigler (1971) even pointed out that the government's control tends to be captured by the existing enterprises in the market, which seek strict control policies by bribing or transferring rents to prevent and restrict the entry of potential enterprises into the market, in order to maintain their monopoly status and high monopoly rents in the market. It is ubiquitous for the government to allocate resources in various countries, where the only difference is the power and coverage of resource allocation, while the formal institution tends to be regarded as an important basis for rigorous restriction and constraint of resource allocation of the government (Klapper et al., 2009). The difference of institutional environment is bound to affect the behavior of the relevant stakeholders in the securities market, such as the external institutional environment of the enterprise affecting its financial statement and other acts (La Porta et al., 1998; Xia & Chen, 2007). This book argues that the financial fraud of organizations under performance pressure will be lowered in the regions with higher institutional efficiency.

First of all, compared with areas with incomplete legal system and low level of law enforcement, the listed companies are more required to provide high-quality financial accounting information in the areas with complete legal system and high level of law enforcement. The more complete the legal system is, the more effective the protection mechanism of investors' interests will be, which will imperceptibly play a role in deterring the enterprise and compel it to be motivated to general certain accounting information with higher quality, thereby making it less likely for the enterprise to engage in earnings operation and financial fraud (Burgstahler & Eames, 2006; Li et al., 2012). Effective implementation of legal supervision system can prevent and reduce earnings operations by enterprises to a certain extent (La Porta, 1998; Ball, 2000; Leuz et al., 2003; Wu & Yu, 2013). The financial statements of listed companies are influenced or constrained by the state of the regional market order and the relevant legal systems, and in the case of disorderly market competition, listed companies are bound to make false propaganda on their financial information so as to cater to investors' market expectations (Che & Qian, 2004; Leuz et al., 2003). The better the institutional environment is and the stricter the law is, the more willing the government is to supervise enterprises, and the fewer financial misrepresentation enterprises will have (Leuz et al., 2003; Bartov & Cohen, 2007; Cohen et al., 2008).

Secondly, the degree of marketization is the main index to measure the construction of regional institutional environment. The better and the faster the marketization in a region is, the more sufficient and the more orderly market competition will be, and the more transparent the market will be, the higher the institutional efficiency will be in the region, and the better the institutional environment will be (Fan, 2010). In this way, the listed companies in the region tend more to improve the quality of financial accounting information through a sound internal control system (Liu et al., 2012). The higher the degree of marketization is in a region, the lower the degree of policy intervention will be, the more transparent it will be, and the less the government will transfer its policy burden to the listed companies, thus reducing the probability of profit manipulation by enterprises in order to conceal the inefficiency of operation. Therefore, the higher the quality of accounting information is, the lower the probability of financial misrepresentation of listed companies will be (Palmrose et al., 2003; Wang, 2010).

Thirdly, from the point of view of the cost of financial litigation and reputation loss, the areas with favorable institutional environment have relatively perfect legal systems and rigorous means of law enforcement, and the enterprise will take high costs of legal litigation for their engagement in false financial statements or financial fraud. Once an enterprise is found to have false financial statements or financial fraud, it will lead to more serious consequences and the loss of reputation of the enterprise and its managers. In this regard, better institutional environment and higher legal risk of financial fraud allow the enterprise and its managers to be better motivated to provide financial reports and accounting information of higher quality (Ball et al., 2000). Studies have shown that firms can gain higher reputation returns by building good reputation, such as helping the firms raise their stock prices (Gomes, 2000) and lower the operating risks (Orlitzky & Benjamin, 2000). On the contrary, the loss of corporate reputation will cause huge losses to the company. For instance, Karpoff & Lott (1993) pointed out that corporate financial fraud would reduce the reputation of the organization and eventually lead to the evaporation of the company's market value. In addition, the enterprise engaged in financial restatements will bear an increasing cost for financing (Newberry & Parthasarathy, 2007). Therefore, in areas with high institutional efficiencies, the possibility of loss of reputation of enterprises and their managers and the cost of violating the law have been significantly increased due to the perfection of the legal system and the strictness of law enforcement. Moreover, even in the face of earnings pressure, enterprises and their managers will not dare to engage in financial fraud in order to maintain the reputation of their own or their organizations.

H9: The better the institutional environment in the area where the enterprise is located is, the lower the degree of illegal financial fraud adopted by the enterprise will be with the increase of its historical performance pressures.

H10: The better the institutional environment in the area where the enterprise is located is, the lower the degree of illegal financial fraud adopted by the enterprise will be with the increase of its industry performance pressures.

According to the above hypotheses, the logical framework of this book is shown in Fig. 3-1. It mainly examines whether enterprises adopt financial fraud under varying degrees of earnings pressure, and what factors of external environment will affect financial fraud of enterprises, and investigates the four factors of political connection of enterprises, financing demand, market competition and institutional environment.

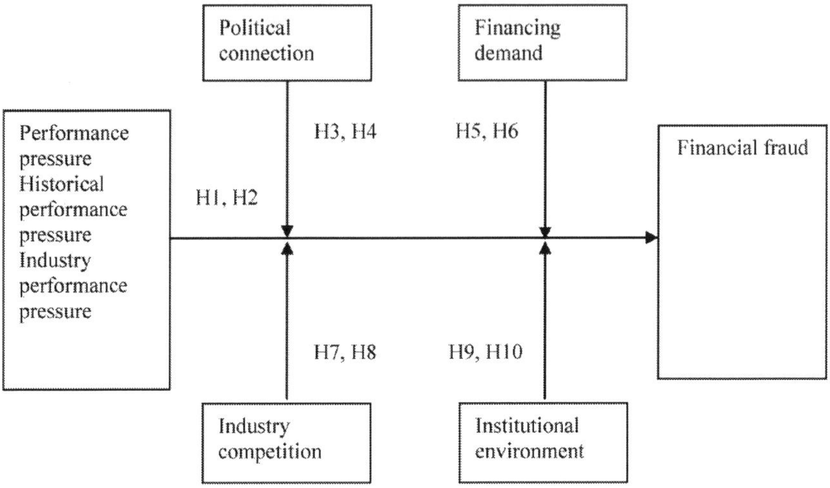

Figure 3-1 Research Model

Chapter 4 Research Design

This chapter mainly introduces the research methods and data sources, and describes in detail the methods of data acquisition and measurement, and designs the corresponding test model according to the theoretical hypotheses in the preceding part.

Research Methods and Data Source

Research Methods

The models and hypotheses in this book show that the research on the relationship between performance pressure and financial fraud of listed companies is in the category of multivariate analysis, while regression analysis is the most commonly used method of multivariate analysis. Therefore, on the basis of the more mature measurement methods in the existing literature, this book mainly used multivariate regression analysis to test the relationship between various variables. Before regression analysis of data, this book first tested the residual values of multiple collinear memory variables of independent variables to ensure that they meet the requirements of normal distribution, error independence, linear relationship and equal variance. In the process of data analysis, descriptive statistics, T-test, correlation analysis and multiple regression analysis were carried out in turn. According to Wu Minglong (2003), Enter is the most appropriate method in research and design if a hypothesis is established in advance to determine the level of importance of variables, while this study conforms to this situation. To be specific, in multivariate regression analysis, this book controlled the order in which each variable enters the regression equation to test the effect of different models. STATA14.0 was used for the processing of all data.

Data Source

The database of this study mainly comes from the samples of listed companies in Shanghai and Shenzhen A-share markets in China. The empirical research methods adopted in this study mainly draw lessons from relevant research at home and abroad. In the existing research literature on financial fraud of listed companies, the COMPUSTAT database of listed companies by the Standard & Poor's is mainly used to study the listed companies of developed countries in Europe and the United States (e.g. http://wrds-web.wharton.upenn.edu/wrds/), while the authoritative databases of listed companies on the Shanghai and Shenzhen A-share markets in China are used to study the listed companies in China, such as CSMAR, WIND and CCER (e.g. http://english.ckgsb.edu.cn/content/csmar; http://www.wind.com.cn/; http://new.ccerdata.cn/). According to the latest statistics of CSMAR, from 2000 to 2015, 92.75% of the research data of 24 top business and economic journals (UTD24) on the corporate governance in China, which were published by University of Texas at Dallas (UT/DALLAS), came from CSMAR, WIND and CCER databases, which reflected the information disclosed by listed companies is reliable and accurate to a certain extent. The data used in this book mainly comes from four databases, among which the data of the key variables, such as financial fraud, performance pressure, corporate performance and enterprise characteristics, mainly comes from CSMAR Database, CCER Economic and Financial Research Database and Wind Database. The data of institutional environment are mainly from NERI INDEX of Marketization of China's Provinces 2011 Report and NERI INDEX of Marketization of China's Provinces 2016 Report published by Fan Gang et al., or the China Governance, Investment Climate, and Harmonious Society: Competitiveness Enhancements for 120 Cities in China published by the World Bank. In order to ensure the accuracy of the data, this study also verified and confirmed the data on some professional websites in China, including http://finance.sina.com.cn/, http: //www.jrj.com, cn/, http: //www.cninfo.com.cn/default.htm and http: //www.cnlist.com/. Details of the sample data are shown in Table 4-1.

Table 4-1 Details of Sample Data

Sample range	**Variable name**	**Data source**
Samples of listed companies in Shanghai and Shenzhen A-share markets	Financial fraud	CSMAR Database; CCER Economic and Financial Research Database
Samples of listed companies in Shanghai and Shenzhen A-share markets	Performance pressure	Wind Database
Samples of listed companies in Shanghai and Shenzhen A-share markets	Political connection	CSMAR Senior Executives Characteristic Database
Samples of listed companies in Shanghai and Shenzhen A-share markets	Institutional environment	NERI INDEX of Marketization
Samples of listed companies in Shanghai and Shenzhen A-share markets	Other control variables	CSMAR Database; CCER Economic and Financial Research Database; Wind Database

In the process of data selection, this study mainly selected the sample of listed companies after 2007, one of the important reasons for which was that, in 2006, the Ministry of Finance of the People's Republic of China issued the Accounting Standards for Business Enterprises --- Basic Standards (2006 Revision) (Order No.33 of the Ministry of Finance), which stipulates that "The Ministry of Finance has amended the Accounting Standards for Enterprises. The amended Accounting Standards for Enterprises – Basic Standards, which were discussed and adopted at the ministerial meeting, are hereby promulgated and shall come into effect as of January 1, 2007." The newly implemented Accounting Standards has made significant adjustments to the disclosure rules of financial information of listed companies (He et al., 2015). In order to make the data consistent, this book established a database of listed companies on the Main Board Market in Shanghai and Shenzhen stock exchanges from 2007 to 2015 by referring to the method of other scholars to take 2007 as the initial point of data collection (Zhang et al., 2015). In this book, according to the topic of this book and the standards of previous scholars, the listed companies were strictly screened to ensure the rationality of sample selection. Specific steps are as follows: (Lian & He, 2014; Lian et al., 2014; Lian et al., 2012):

1) Exclude the samples of listed financial companies, banks, securities companies, insurance companies and other financially regulated companies;

2) Exclude companies whose nature can not be determined;

3) Exclude samples with abnormalities in the financial situation of ST shares (Special Treatment) and PT shares (Particular Transfer);

4) Exclude the samples of companies whose data has serious deficiencies.

Finally, a total of 6,903 observations between 2007 and 2015 were obtained.

Variable Measurement and Testing Model

Independent Variables

Performance pressure: The traditional definition of performance pressure is that the actual performance of an enterprise is lower than the expected level predicted by an analyst, which is mainly measured by the difference between the actual performance level of an enterprise and the expected level predicted by an analyst, while the greater the difference is, the heavier the performance pressure of the enterprise will be (Kasznik & McNichols, 2002). However, in this study, because financial fraud may occur in listed companies, it can not reflect the true performance of the enterprise with the real earnings per share (EPS), but the ROA (return on assets) can give a more accurate result of the actual performance of the enterprise (Fung, 2015). Fung (2015) believes that the corporate performance pressures of managers mainly come from two aspects of comparison, the gap between the actual performance of the enterprise and its competitors and the gap between the actual performance of the enterprise and its historical performance. Chen (2008) also holds that performance pressures of enterprises are mainly composed of historical performance pressure and industry performance pressure. Among the studies of prospect theory, some scholars believe that the performance pressure of enterprises should be combined with the historical performance pressure and the industry performance pressure to predict managers' behavior decisions, which will provide the enterprises with more information (Baum et al., 2005; Greve, 2005; Kim & Gaba, 2015), in which the performance pressure is calculated by giving different weights to the two parts. Some other scholars hold that historical performance pressures and industry performance pressures are two different references for managers, while the pressure on managers comes from the differences in the mechanisms, and varied pressure may lead to the disparity in the decision-making of managers, thereby making it necessary to calculate and compare the two indexes separately (Chen, 2008; Greve, 2008; Joseph & Gaba, 2015). In this study, the author makes a strict distinction between historical performance pressure and industrial performance pressure of enterprises.

Historical Performance Pressure ($\boldsymbol{HP_{i,t}}$)

The measurement of historical performance pressures is mainly based on Greve's (2008) research, which is calculated as follows:

$$HP_{i,t} = P_{i,t-1} - HA_{i,t-1}$$

In the formula, $P_{i,t-1}$ refers to the actual performance (ROA)[①] of the enterprise i in the period t-1, and $HA_{i,t-1}$ refers to the historical expected performance of the enterprise i in the period t-1. The difference between them is the historical performance pressure of the enterprise. According to Greve (2008), the calculation formula of $HA_{i,t-1}$ is as follows:

$$HA_{i,t-1} = (1 - \alpha)P_{i,t-2} + \alpha HA_{i,t-2}$$

In the formula, α refers to the weight, ranging from 0 to 1, which is assigned for each increase of 0.1, and then the different values of $HA_{i,t-1}$ were used to test the robustness. Referring to the research by Chen(2008), the author only reported the result when α was 0.4. Hence, the historical expected performance of the enterprise i during the period t-1 $HA_{i,t-1}$ was the weighted moving average between the actual performance of the enterprise i during the period t-2 (weight 0.6) and the historical expected performance during the period t-2 (weight 0.4). Thus, the historical performance pressure of the enterprise ($\boldsymbol{HP_{i,t}}$) is the

---

① It should be pointed out that it is based on the computing formula of ROA: ROA = Net profit / average total assets * 100%. To facilitate calculation and processing, the percent signs of the values of all the variables involved in this book, which are based on ROA, are removed and calculated directly according to the numerical value.

difference between $P_{i,t-1}$ and $HA_{i,t-1}$ $(P_{i,t-1} - HA_{i,t-1})$. When it is $(P_{i,t-1} - HA_{i,t-1})>0$, it shows that the actual performance of the enterprise will be higher than its historical expected performance, and then its managers will not suffer any performance pressure. When it is $(P_{i,t-1} - HA_{i,t-1})<0$, it shows that the actual performance of the enterprise will be lower than its historical expected performance. Further, we process the end of $(P_{i,t-1} - HA_{i,t-1})$ to define the dummy variable I_1. When it is that $(P_{i,t-1} - HA_{i,t-1})<0$, I_1 is assigned as 1, and then the historical performance pressure of the enterprise is as follows:

$$HP_{i,t} = I_1 \left| P_{i,t-1} - HA_{i,t-1} \right|$$

$I_1 = 1$, if$(P_{i,t-1} - HA_{i,t-1})<0$

$I_1 = 0$, if$(P_{i,t-1} - HA_{i,t-1})>0$

Industry Performance Pressure ($\boldsymbol{IP_{i,t}}$)

Similarly, industry performance pressure is mainly measured based on the research of Greve (2008) and Markus and Brauer (2012), which is calculated as follows:

$$IP_{i,t} = P_{i,t-1} - SA_{i,t-1}$$

In the formula, $P_{i,t-1}$ represents the actual performance of the enterprise i in the period t-1 (ROA), $SA_{i,t-1}$ represents the industry expected performance of the enterprise i in the period t-1, and the difference between the two is the industry performance pressure of the enterprise. In the same way, $SA_{i,t-1}$ is calculated as follows:

$$SA_{i,t-1} = (1 - \alpha)P_{i,t-2} + \alpha SA_{i,t-2}$$

In the formula, α refers to the weight, ranging from 0 to 1, which is assigned for each increase of 0.1, and then the different values of $SA_{i,t-1}$ were used to test the robustness. Referring to the research by Chen(2008), the author only reported the result when α was 0.4. Hnece, the historical expected performance of the enterprise i during the period t-1 $SA_{i,t-1}$ was the weighted moving average between the actual performance of the enterprise i during the period t-2 (weight 0.6) and the historical expected performance during the period t-2 (weight 0.4). Thus, the industry performance pressure of the enterprise ($\boldsymbol{IP_{i,t}}$) is the difference between $P_{i,t-1}$ and $HA_{i,t-1}$ $(P_{i,t-1} - HA_{i,t-1})$. When it is $(P_{i,t-1} - SA_{i,t-1})>0$, it shows that the actual performance of the enterprise will be higher than its industry expected performance, and then its managers will not suffer any industry performance pressure. When it is that $(P_{i,t-1} - SA_{i,t-1})<0$, it shows that the actual performance of the enterprise will be lower than its industry expected performance. Further, we process the end of $(P_{i,t-1} - SA_{i,t-1})$ to define the dummy variable I_1. When it is that $(P_{i,t-1} - SA_{i,t-1})<0$, I_1 is assigned as 1, and then the industry performance pressure of the enterprise is as follows:

$$IP_{i,t} = I_1 \left| P_{i,t-1} - SA_{i,t-1} \right|$$

$I_1 = 1, \text{if}(P_{i,t-1} - SA_{i,t-1})<0$

$I_1 = 0, \text{if}(P_{i,t-1} - SA_{i,t-1})>0$

Dependent Variable

Financial Fraud (FR)

Financial fraud refers to the behavior that enterprises manipulate their financial information for personal gain by making false accounts and preparing false accounting statements in the process of accounting. Moreover, it refers to the deliberate misrepresentation of certain financial values and exaggeration of the profitability of enterprises, so as to deceive shareholders, creditors and other stakeholders. From the perspective of accounting information reflected, financial fraud is mainly manifested in two types, false accounting events and false accounting statements. According to the above definition, the following indicators were collected in this book to measure financial information fraud, including fictitious profits (times), fictitious assets (times), false records (times), misleading statements (times), delayed disclosure (times), major omissions (times), and false disclosure (times). The basic data of the above-mentioned financial information fraud were manually collated according to the information in the Database of Illegal Acts in CASMR Database. In this study, the author mainly measured financial fraud in the following two ways. The first way is to sum up the number of financial fraud actions the enterprise had in the same year, and the greater the index is, the higher the degree of fraud of financial information in the same year will be (He et al., 2015). The other way is to use dummy variable, where an enterprise with the above financial frauds is assigned as 1, otherwise it will be assigned as 0. In subsequent empirical research, the author will adopt the former as the major method for analysis, and the latter for robustness test.

Moderating Variable

The moderating variables in this study mainly involve variables at the organizational, industrial and regional levels, among which the moderating variables at the organizational level mainly include political connection and financing demand, those at the industrial level include the degree of industry competition, and those at the regional level include regional institutional environment.

Political Connection (PL)

There are three main types of representative measurement criteria for corporate political connection in existing studies:

The first type is based on the relationship between the enterprise and the family of political figures. For instance, in the study of listed companies in Indonesia, Fisman (2001) defined all the listed companies which were associated with members of the Suharto family as companies with political connections.

The second type is based on the association between senior executives in enterprises and government officials. Taking a typical case, Faccio (2006) took companies from 47 countries as samples and defined political connection as the basic criterion for judging whether a company has political connection is that the company must have at least one major owner (in direct or indirect control of the at least 10% of the voting rights of the company), or its senior executives are kings, presidents, prime ministers or have direct and close ties with a senior government official and political party.

The third is based on the service of senior executives of enterprises in government agencies. Betrend et al. (2004) argued that, in France, the CEO of a company who graduates from an elite school and holds a position in a key government department is deemed to have political connection. The third is divided by the company's donations to political parties, such as Goledman (2006) and Claessens et al. (2006). In consideration of the stipulation that excellent private entrepreneurs have been allowed to join the Party since the revision of the Constitution in the Sixteenth National Congress of the Communist Party of China, it has become an important way for entrepreneurs to participate in the administration and discussion of state affairs by assuming the office of deputies to the NPC and members of the CPPCC. Based on the research of Luo Danglun et al. (2015), this book mainly investigates whether the CEO or other TMT (top management team) members of an enterprise act as deputies to the NPC and members of the CPPCC. If the CEO or other TMT members act as deputies to the NPC and members of the CPPCC, PL is set as 1, otherwise it will be 0.

Financing Demand (RZ)

The expected total investment of the company is obtained by adding the expected annual normal additional investment rate of the company to the estimated sustainable investment expressed by the accumulated depreciation and amortization in the same year (divided by the company's total assets at the beginning of the year for standardization). After subtracting the difference of net cash flow in the company's annual operating activities (divided by its total assets at the beginning of the year for standardization), the internal cash gap of the company's investment expenditure in this year can be obtained as the financing amount. In this study, the author mainly refers to the calculation method proposed by Demirgu-Kunt and Maksimovic (1998), which regards the difference between enterprise growth and achievable endogenous growth as financing demand. The larger the value is, the higher the financing demand of the enterprise will be. The calculation formula is as follows:

$$RZ = \frac{A_{i,t} - A_{i,t-1}}{A_{i,t-1}} - \frac{ROE_{i,t}}{1 - ROE_{i,t}}$$

In the formula, A represents the asset scale of enterprises and ROE represents the return on equity. On this basis, the FN larger than the annual mean value of the industry is represented as 1, otherwise it will be represented as 0.

Degree of Industry Competition (JZ)

So far, there is no consensus on the measurement of the degree of industry competition. n economics, market competition intensity is mainly measured by the characteristics of market structure, such as product differentiation, concentration, average profit rate in the market, the number of enterprises in the market and barriers to entry and so forth. The most widely used measurement method in existing research is the Herfindahl Index (HHI) of the industry (He et al., 2016; Li et al., 2015), which is calculated as follows:

$$HHI = \sum_{t=1}^{n} \left(\frac{X_i}{X}\right)^2$$

$$X = \sum_{t=1}^{n} X_i$$

In the formula, X_i represents the sales revenue of the enterprise i, and n represents the number of enterprises in the market. HHI can better reflect the market concentration. The lower the HHI is, the smaller the difference of sales volume among enterprises in the market will be, the lower the market concentration will be and the higher the market competition will be. The higher the HHI is, the larger the difference of sales volume among enterprises in the market will be, the higher the market concentration will be and the lower the market competition will be.

Institutional Environment (IN

Institutional environment is mainly measured based on NERI INDEX of Marketization of China's Provinces Report compiled by Fan Gang et al. The higher the marketization index is, the higher the degree of marketization or institutional efficiencies of the regional environment in which the organization is located will be.

Control Variable

For the choice of control variable, this study mainly chose the variables from the organizational level and the industry level, and controlled the factors that may have an impact on the financial fraud of enterprises by combining the existing relevant literature.

At the organizational level, the author mainly controls the following variables:

(1) Enterprise age (*NL*): It is the logarithm of the years that the enterprise is actually established.

(2) Enterprise scale (*GM*): Enterprise scale is mainly measured in two ways, one of which is based on the number of employees in enterprises. However, due to the large differences in the number of employees employed in different industries, the natural logarithm of the company's total assets at the end of the term was adopted in this study.

(3) Ownership concentration (*GQ*): The ownership concentration was measured by the method proposed by Yang Jianjun et al. (2015) and

by the HHI of the shareholding ratio of the top five substantial shareholders.

(4) Organizational slack (*RY*): The organizational slack of an enterprise can be divided into absorbed slack and unabsorbed slack according to the degree of free domination and the degree of flexibility. Since the absorbed slack is strongly dependent on the situation and the start-ups are able to fully identify the specific resources necessary for their growth, the start-ups have a stronger demand for unabsorbed organizational slack with higher redistribution flexibility. To be specific, unabsorbed slack refers to the resources that can be mobilized by enterprises in a short time, which mean the existing resources for which enterprises have not specified specific purposes, such as reserve funds, retained earnings of enterprises, and so forth. As for the measurement method, the author measures the organizational slack with the potential slack, namely, the ratio of liabilities to assets, which is represented by the reciprocal of the ratio of assets to liabilities (Singh, 1986; Peng et al., 2010; Zou & Ni, 2010; Li & Liu, 2010). The higher the asset-liability ratio is, the fewer organizational slack the enterprise will have, the weaker abilities the start-ups will have to obtain funds by increasing their liabilities, and the lower the ability of resource redistribution will be.

(5) Separation of chairman and CEO (*LZ*): Krause (2014) divided separation of chairman and CEO into three categories, apprentice-based separation (Apprentice), departure-based separation (Departure) and demotion-based separation (Demotion). In this study, the author assigns a value of 1 to the case where the chairman and the CEO are the same person, otherwise the value is set to 0.

(6) Ratio of independent directors (*DD*): The ratio of independent directors is defined as the proportion of external independent directors to the number of board members.

(7) Shareholding ratio of senior executives (*CG*): It refers to the proportion of shares held by top managers to total equity.

In addition, this book also set annual dummy variables (NF) to control the influence of annual change trend on enterprise decision-making behavior, taking into account the influence of industry differences on enterprise decision-making behavior. The control variable of industry factor (IND) was designed according to the industry classification of China Securities Regulatory Commission, and the dummy variable was designed based on the standards of the three-level industry classification. It involved 27 industries, so that 26 industry dummy variables were designed. Finally, in order to control the annual factors of the observed data, annual dummy variables were designed. Since the data was observed for seven years, six annual dummy variables were designed. The details of variable design and measurement methods are shown in Table 4-2.

Table 4-2 Definitions and Measurements of Variables

Variable name	Abbreviation	Definition	Measurement method	**Variable operation**
Dependent variable				
Financial fraud	*FR*	Financial fraud refers to the intentional misstatement or omission of important facts, or the provision of misleading accounting data, and the provision of accounting data that, when considered in conjunction with all other available information, may lead users to change their judgments and decisions (ACFE, 1993).	Behaviors such as fictitious profits (times), fictitious assets (times), false records (times), misleading statements (times), delayed disclosure (times), major omissions (times), false disclosure (times)	Coding of raw data

Variable name	Abbreviation	Definition	Measurement method	**Variable operation**
Independent variable				
Historical performance pressure	*HP*	It reflects the gap between current actual performance and historical expected performance of enterprises (Chen, 2008).	The gap between current actual performance and historical expected performance of enterprises	$HP_{i,t} = I_1\|P_{i,t-1} - HA_{i,t-1}\|$
Industry performance pressure	*IP*	It reflects the gap between current actual performance and expected industry performance of enterprises (Greve, 2008; Joseph & Gaba, 2015).	The gap between current actual performance and expected industry performance of enterprises	$IP_{i,t} = I_1\|P_{i,t-1} - SA_{i,t-1}\|$
Moderating variable				
Political connection	*PL*	Enterprise managers actively or passively establish a special relationship with the government by investing resources (Faccio, 2006; Luo, 2009; Tian & Zhang, 2013).	It mainly inspects whether the CEO or other TMT members of an enterprise act as deputies to the NPC and members of the CPPCC.	Coding of raw data

Variable name	Abbreviation	Definition	Measurement method	**Variable operation**
Financing demand	*RZ*	It refers to the internal cash gap of the company's investment expenditure this year (Teoh et al., 1998; Li et al., 2011).	It is measured by the difference between enterprise growth and achievable endogenous growth.	$RZ = \frac{A_{i,t} - A_{i,t-1}}{A_{i,t-1}} - \frac{ROE_{i,t}}{1 - ROE_{i,t}}$
Degree of industry competition	*JZ*	It refers to the degree of competition in the industry in which the enterprise is located (Boeker, 1997; Wiersema &Bantel, 1992).	It is measured by Herfindahl index.	$HHI = \sum_{t=1}^{n} \left(\frac{X_i}{X}\right)^2$
Institutional environment	*IN*	It measures the degree of marketization in different regions.	It is measured by NERI INDEX of Marketization by Fan Gang.	Coding of raw data
Control variable				
Enterprise age	*NL*	It controls the influence of enterprise age on its strategic choice.	It is measured by the logarithm of the difference from the year of data observation minus the year of the establishment of the enterprise.	Coding of raw data
Enterprise scale	*GM*	It controls the impact of enterprise scale on its engagement in financial fraud.	It is measured by the natural logarithm of total assets.	Coding of raw data

Variable name	Abbreviation	Definition	Measurement method	**Variable operation**
Ownership concentration	*GQ*	It controls the influence of enterprises' ownership concentration on managers' strategic decision-making under performance pressure.	It is measured by the Herfindahl index of the shareholding ratio of the top five substantial shareholders.	Coding of raw data
Organizational slack	*RY*	It controls the influence of enterprises' organizational slack on managers' strategic decision-making under performance pressure.	It is measured by the outcome of dividing total liabilities by total assets.	Coding of raw data
Separation of chairman and CEO	*LZ*	It controls the influence of the separation of chairman and CEO between managers and decision makers on strategic decision-making of enterprises.	It checks whether the chairman and CEO are the same person.	Coding of raw data
Ratio of independent directors	*DD*	It controls the influence of the external supervision of independent directors on the strategic decision-making of enterprises.	It is measured by the proportion of the number of external independent directors to the number of board members.	Coding of raw data

Variable name	Abbreviation	Definition	Measurement method	**Variable operation**
Shareholding ratio of senior executives	*GG*	It controls the impact of the shareholding ratio of senior executives on their strategic decision-making.	It is measured by the proportion of shares held by top managers to total equity.	Coding of raw data
Industry type	*IND*	It controls the differences in the characteristics of different industries.	It is measured by the subdivided industry where the enterprise is located (dummy variable).	Design dummy variable according to industry type
Annual variable	*NF*	It controls the impact of operating periods on financial fraud.	It is measured by the year when the data is observed (dummy variable).	Design dummy variable according to different years

Hypothesis Testing Model

In order to test hypotheses H1 and H2 for the main effects of this study, the following models were constructed to be tested:

$$FR_{i,t} = \beta_0 + \beta_1 HP_{i,t} + \sum_{i=1}^{n} \alpha_i \times Control_i + \delta \quad (1)$$

$$FR_{i,t} = \beta_0 + \beta_1 IP_{i,t} + \sum_{i=1}^{n} \alpha_i \times Control_i + \delta \quad (2)$$

In the Model 1 and 2, FR represents the financial fraud of the enterprise i in the year t, HP and IP represent historical performance pressure and industry performance pressure of the enterprise, Control represents all control variables, including enterprise age(*NL*), enterprise scale(*GM*), ownership concentration(*GQ*), organizational slack(*RY*), separation of chairman and CEO(*LZ*), ratio of independent directors(*DD*), shareholding ratio of senior executives(*CG*), annual dummy variables(*NF*), and industry dummy variable. δ represents the residual.

In order to test the hypotheses H3 – H10 for moderating effect, the following models were constructed to be tested:

$$FR_{i,t} = \beta_0 + \beta_1 HP_{i,t} + \beta_2 HP_{i,t} \times PL + \beta_3 PL + \sum_{i=1}^{n} \alpha_i \times Control_i + \delta \quad (3)$$

$$FR_{i,t} = \beta_0 + \beta_1 IP_{i,t} + \beta_2 IP_{i,t} \times PL + \beta_3 PL + \sum_{i=1}^{n} \alpha_i \times Control_i + \delta \quad (4)$$

$$FR_{i,t} = \beta_0 + \beta_1 HP_{i,t} + \beta_2 HP_{i,t} \times RZ + \beta_3 RZ + \sum_{i=1}^{n} \alpha_i \times Control_i + \delta \quad (5)$$

$$FR_{i,t} = \beta_0 + \beta_1 IP_{i,t} + \beta_2 IP_{i,t} \times RZ + \beta_3 RZ + \sum_{i=1}^{n} \alpha_i \times Control_i + \delta \quad (6)$$

$$FR_{i,t} = \beta_0 + \beta_1 HP_{i,t} + \beta_2 HP_{i,t} \times JZ + \beta_3 JZ + \sum_{i=1}^{n} \alpha_i \times Control_i + \delta \quad (7)$$

$$FR_{i,t} = \beta_0 + \beta_1 IP_{i,t} + \beta_2 IP_{i,t} \times JZ + \beta_3 JZ + \sum_{i=1}^{n} \alpha_i \times Control_i + \delta \quad (8)$$

$$FR_{i,t} = \beta_0 + \beta_1 HP_{i,t} + \beta_2 HP_{i,t} \times IN + \beta_3 IN + \sum_{i=1}^{n} \alpha_i \times Control_i + \delta \quad (9)$$

$$FR_{i,t} = \beta_0 + \beta_1 IP_{i,t} + \beta_2 IP_{i,t} \times IN + \beta_3 IN + \sum_{i=1}^{n} \alpha_i \times Control_i + \delta \quad (10)$$

$$FR_{i,t} = \beta_0 + \beta_1 HP_{i,t} + \beta_2 HP_{i,t} \times PL + \beta_2 HP_{i,t} \times RZ + \beta_3 HP_{i,t} \times JZ + \beta_4 HP_{i,t} \times IN + \beta_5 PL + \beta_6 RZ + \beta_7 JZ + +\beta_8 IN + \sum_{i=1}^{n} \alpha_i \times Control_i + \delta \quad (11)$$

$$FR_{i,t} = \beta_0 + \beta_1 IP_{i,t} + \beta_2 IP_{i,t} \times PL + \beta_2 IP_{i,t} \times RZ + \beta_2 IP_{i,t} \times JZ + \beta_2 IP_{i,t} \times IN + \beta_5 PL + \beta_6 RZ + \beta_7 JZ + +\beta_8 IN + \sum_{i=1}^{n} \alpha_i \times Control_i + \delta \quad (12)$$

In the Model 3 – 10, FR represents the financial fraud of the enterprise i in the year t, HP and IP represent historical performance pressure and industry performance pressure of the enterprise, PL, RZ, JZ, IN represent the moderating variables, political connection, financing demand, degree of industry competition and regional institutional environment. Control represents all control variables, including enterprise age(*NL*), enterprise scale(*GM*), ownership concentration(*GQ*), organizational slack(*RY*), separation of chairman and CEO(*LZ*), ratio of independent directors(*DD*), shareholding ratio of senior executives(*CG*), annual dummy variables(*NF*), and industry dummy variable. δ represents the residual.

Equations 3 and 4 test the moderating effect of political connection on the relationship between historical performance pressure, industry performance pressures and financial fraud of the enterprises, respectively. Equations 5 and 6 test the moderating effect of financing demand on the relationship between historical performance pressure, industry performance pressures and financial fraud of the enterprises, respectively. Equations 7 and 8 test the moderating effect of the degree of industry competition on the relationship between historical performance pressure, industry performance pressures and financial fraud of the enterprises, respectively. Equations 9 and 10 test the moderating effect of institutional environment on the relationship between historical performance pressure, industry performance pressures and financial fraud of the enterprises, respectively. Equations 11 and 12 are full models.

Chapter 5 Hypothesis Testing and Result Analysis

According to the research hypothesis proposed in the previous theoretical construction and the sample data mined, this chapter mainly carried on the systematic analysis to the data. Firstly, descriptive statistical analysis of the original measurement variables was carried out, and their distribution characteristics were roughly described, and the data quality was observed. On this basis, the mean values of different groups were compared according to the relevant grouping variables, and their differences were analyzed. Secondly, according to the definition and measurement method of variables, the initial variables were processed and the corresponding research variables were constructed. Finally, the corresponding statistical model was analyzed, the theoretical hypotheses were tested, and the results were summarized and further analyzed.

Descriptive Statistical Analysis

Descriptive Statistics of Variables

Table 5-1 mainly describes the industry distribution of the research samples. According to the table, the samples are mostly distributed in manufacturing industry, accounting for 58.38%, followed by electronic information technology industry, accounting for 7.96%, and then wholesale and retail trades, accounting for 6.47%. The agriculture, forestry, animal husbandry and fishery account for the least proportion.

Table 5-1 Industry Distribution of Samples

Industry code	Proportion	Observed value	Industry
IND1	0.0132	91	Agriculture, forestry, animal husbandry and fishery
IND2	0.0225	155	Mining and quarrying
IND3	0.5838	4,030	Manufacturing industry
IND4	0.0456	315	Production and supply of electricity, water and gas
IND5	0.0258	178	Construction
IND6	0.0439	303	Transportation and warehousing industries
IND7	0.0796	549	Electronic information technology industry
IND8	0.0647	447	Wholesale and retail trades
IND9	0.0438	302	Real estate industry
IND10	0.0341	235	Social service industry
IND11	0.0172	119	Information and cultural industries
IND12	0.0258	178	Comprehensive industry

Table 5-2 mainly describes the regional distribution of research samples. From the perspective of sample distribution, the areas with the largest number of samples are mainly in the southern coastal areas, accounting for 51.34%, more than half of total samples. Secondly, it is mainly concentrated in the Bohai Rim Region, accounting for 16.22%. Then it is Central China, accounting for 10.90%, Southwest China, accounting for 9.22%, Northeast China, accounting for 4.24%, and Northwest China, accounting for 0.8%. Through the industry and region distribution of samples, it can be seen that the distribution of samples is highly in line with the basic situation of Listed Companies in China, which indicates that there is no serious deviation in the selection of samples.

Table 5-2 Regional Distribution of Samples

Geographical area	**Proportion**	**Observed value**	**Region and Province**
Southeast China	0.5134	3,544	Jiangsu, Shanghai, Zhejiang, Fujian and Guangdong
The Bohai Rim Region	0.235	1,622	Shandong, Beijing, Tianjin and Hebei
Central China	0.109	752	Anhui, Henan, Hubei, Hunan and Jiangxi
Northeast China	0.0424	293	Heilongjiang, Jilin, and Liaoning
Southwest China	0.0922	636	Yunnan, Guizhou, Guangxi, Sichuan, Chongqing and Hainan
Northwest China	0.008	55	Shanxi, Shaanxi, Inner Mongolia, Ningxia, Qinghai, Gansu and Xinjiang

Notes: The regions are divided according to NBS (National Bureau of Statistics), and the details of division rules are shown in http://data.stats.gov.cn/

Table 5-3 is mainly about the descriptive statistics of key variables in the study. Through descriptive statistics, it can be found that mean value of dependent variable definition fraud (FR) was 0.126 with a standard error of 0.558, mean value of enterprises' historical performance pressure (HP) was 0.278 with a standard error of 0.362, and mean value of enterprises' industry performance pressure (IP) was 0.156 with a standard error of 0. 578. In all samples, 9.80% of the listed companies have political connections, which indicates that there is a certain proportion of the listed companies with CEO or senior executives who are deputies to the NPC or members of the CPPCC.

Table 5-3 Descriptive Statistics of Key Variables

Variables	*Obs*	*Mean*	*Std.Dev*	*Min*	*Max*
FR	6903	0.226	0.558	0.000	6.000
HP	6903	0.278	0.362	0.000	4.278
IP	6903	0.156	0.578	0.000	11.428
PL	6903	0.098	0.395	0.000	1.000
RZ	6903	0. 344	0.475	0.000	1.000
JZ	6903	0.117	0.129	0.149	1.000
IN	6903	6.213	2.548	3.54	11.800
NL	6903	2.657	0.468	2.15	3.880
GM	6903	12.780	1.534	18.69	25.590
GQ	6903	36.350	14.48	3.105	84.48
RY	6903	0.157	5.143	-1.258	420.18
LZ	6903	0.258	0.442	0.000	1.000
DD	6903	0.305	0.064	0.000	0.750
GG	6903	0.073	0.152	0.000	0.872

Correlation Analysis of Variables

Table 5-4 mainly reports the correlation coefficient table of variables, from which it can be found that there is a significant positive correlation between historical performance pressure and financial fraud of enterprises (beta=0. 205, p<0.01), and that there is a significant positive correlation between industry performance pressure and financial fraud of enterprises (beta=0. 106, p<0.01), which preliminarily supports the related hypothesis. It can be further found that there is a significant positive correlation between corporate political connection and financial fraud (beta=0. 067, p<0.05), a significant positive correlation between corporate financing demand and financial fraud (beta=0. 136, p<0.01) and a significant negative correlation between institutional environment in the region where the enterprise is located and financial fraud (beta=0. 179, p<0.01).

Table 5-4 Correlation Coefficient Table of Key Variables (N=6,903)

Variables	*1*	*2*	*3*	*4*	*5*	*6*	*7*
1.FR	1.000						
2.HP	0.205	1.000					
3.IP	0.106	0.074	1.000				
4.PL	0.067	0.053	0.125	1.000			
5.RZ	0.136	0.036	0.063	0.073	1.000		
6.JZ	0.021	0.105	0.017	0.042	-0.068	1.000	
7.IN	-0.179	0.126	0.224	0.014	-0.051	0.032	1.000
8.NL	0.010	-0.067	0.251	0.008	0.236	0.175	-0.008
9.GM	-0.044	0.087	-0.006	0.180	0.027	0.022	0.032
10.GQ	0.027	0.113	0.148	-0.043	-0.251	-0.262	0.034
11.RY	0.140	-0.021	-0.183	0.017	0.169	-0.237	-0.033
12.LZ	0.067	0.064	0.079	0.055	-0.124	-0.142	0.106
13.DD	-0.064	0.058	0.007	0.227	0.168	0.017	0.023
14.GG	0.005	0.008	0.107	-0.044	0.090	0.088	0.017
Variables	***8***	***9***	***10***	***11***	***12***	***13***	***14***
8.NL	1.000						
9.GM	0.093	1.000					
10.GQ	-0.062	-0.133	1.000				
11.RY	0.187	0.105	-0.194	1.000			
12.LZ	-0.013	-0.072	0.157	-0.062	1.000		
13.DD	0.034	0.046	0.176	-0.106	0.102	1.000	
14.GG	0.031	-0.115	0.003	0.074	0.118	0.102	1.000

Notes: N=6,903; Variables with absolute value of correlation coefficient above 0.055 are significant at 0.05 level, and those with absolute value of correlation coefficient greater than 0.067 are significant at P=0.01 level. Industry and year dummy variables are included.

Hypothesis Testing and Analysis

Before the specific test, the data were processed as follows to ensure the consistency and validity of the model estimation. Firstly, in order to avoid the influence of outliers on the test results, Winsorize was applied to the main continuous variables at 1% level (Flannery & Rangan, 2006). Secondly, in order to avoid the influence of multiple collinearity, the continuous variables measured by the interaction term were centralized (He et al., 2010). In addition, Variance Inflation Factor (VIF) was used to diagnose all explanatory variables. The results show that the variance of all explanatory variables is between 68% and 90% independent of other explanatory variables, with an average VIF of 3.200, which can eliminate the problem of multiple collinearity. Thirdly, the data in this book are panel data, which may have some problems, such as heteroscedasticity, temporal correlation and cross-sectional correlation. The standard error will be underestimated by using the common panel data estimation methods, which results in certain deviation in the results of model estimation, but the standard error estimated by Driscoll-Kraay standard deviation is unbiased, consistent and effective (Driscoll & Kraay, 1998). Therefore, in the following panel data model estimation, the D-K standard error method is used for estimation. Moreover, in order to ensure the robustness of the test results, the standard errors were tested by means of the enterprise-level Cluster adjustment (Yu et al., 2010), Bootstrap self-sampling method and Robust heteroscedastic robustness method.

The empirical analysis ideas of this study are as follows:

First, the relationship between corporate historical performance pressure, industry performance pressure and financial fraud is examined;

Second, the moderating effects of the political connection, financing demand, industry competition and institutional environment on the relationship between the two types of performance pressures and financial fraud are tested;

Finally, the robustness test is carried out by replacing the key variables.

Test of the Relationship between Performance Pressure and Financial Fraud

Table 5-5 reports the test of the relationship between corporate performance pressure and financial fraud. Model 1 in Table 5-5 is the benchmark model, including all control variables, Model 2 includes all control variables and moderating variables, Model 3 is a test model with independent variable historical performance pressure, Model 4 is a test model with independent variable industry performance pressure and Model 5 is a full model. The results of Model 3 show that there is a significant positive correlation between enterprise historical performance pressure and financial fraud (beta= 0.085, $P < 0.001$), indicating that the greater the historical performance pressure of the enterprise is, the higher the degree of financial fraud that the enterprise engages in will be. Therefore, H1 was verified. The results of Model 4 show that there is a significant positive correlation between corporate industry performance pressure and financial fraud (beta= 0.199, $P < 0.01$), indicating that, the greater the industry performance pressure of the enterprise is, the higher the degree of financial fraud that the enterprise engages in will be. Therefore, H2 was verified. The above results still maintain fairly good robustness in the Model 5.

Table 5-5 Test of the Relationship between Corporate Performance Pressure and Financial Fraud

Variables	*FR*				
	M1	M2	M3	M4	M5
HP			0.085***		0.069***
			(0.022)		(0.025)
IP				0.199**	0.136*
				(0.061)	(0.057)
NL	0.190***	0.186***	-0.361***	-0.359***	0.183***
	(0.036)	(0.033)	(0.031)	(0.030)	(0.036)
GM	0.015	0.015	0.187***	0.186***	0.0172
	(0.017)	(0.019)	(0.030)	(0.029)	(0.017)

Variables	***FR***				
	M1	M2	M3	M4	M5
GQ	-0.001	-0.001	-0.000	-0.000	-0.000
	(0.000)	(0.000)	(0.000)	(0.000)	(0.000)
RY	-0.032***	-0.032***	-0.024***	-0.024***	-0.024***
	(0.008)	(0.007)	(0.005)	(0.005)	(0.005)
LZ	0.021***	0.017***	-0.005	-0.005	-0.004
	(0.004)	(0.004)	(0.005)	(0.005)	(0.005)
DD	0.118***	0.118***	0.286***	0.281***	0.273***
	(0.032)	(0.032)	(0.035)	(0.036)	(0.033)
GG	0.032+	0.032+	0.007	0.008	0.008
	(0.017)	(0.018)	(0.010)	(0.011)	(0.011)
PL		0.011**	0.053***	0.054***	0.010**
		(0.004)	(0.007)	(0.007)	(0.004)
RZ		0.016***	0.004**	0.004**	0.016***
		(0.003)	(0.002)	(0.002)	(0.003)
JZ		0.353	-0.133	-0.117	0.406
		(0.294)	(0.180)	(0.186)	(0.272)
IN		-0.336***	-0.0223	-0.091**	0.230***
		(0.042)	(0.074)	(0.043)	(0.088)
_Cons	0.907***	0.929***	0.623***	0.592***	0.589***
	(0.100)	(0.101)	(0.063)	(0.064)	(0.062)
IND	Control	Control	Control	Control	Control
NF	Control	Control	Control	Control	Control
F	446.355^{***}	202.021^{***}	420.510^{***}	366.892^{***}	67.513^{***}
Adj_R^2	0.023	0.024	0.026	0.027	0.028
N	6903	6903	6903	6903	6903

Notes: $^{+}$P<0.1, *P<0.05, **P<0.01, ***P<0.001,the values in brackets are adjusted standard errors.

Rational Test of Moderating Effect

Table 5-6 reports the moderating effect test of the relationship between corporate performance pressure and financial fraud. Model 1 includes all control variables and moderating variables. Model 2 tests the moderating effect of political connection on the relationship between performance pressure and financial fraud, reflecting that political connection can promote the positive correlation between historical performance pressure and financial fraud (beta= 0.063, $P < 0.001$), and also boost the positive correlation between industry performance pressure and financial fraud (beta= 0.095, $P < 0.01$). Compared with the enterprises without political connection, the greater historical performance pressure and industry performance pressure the enterprise with political connection is faced with, the more financial fraud it will engage in. Therefore, H3 and H4 were verified.

The results of Model 3 show that financing demand can promote the positive correlation between enterprise historical performance pressure and financial fraud (beta= 0.113, $P < 0.001$), but the moderating effect of financing demand on the positive correlation between industry performance pressure and financial fraud is not significant. Compared with enterprises with lower financing demand, the greater historical performance pressure the enterprise with higher financing demand is faced with, the more financial fraud it will engage in. Thus, H5 was verified. However, the intensity of corporate financing demand does not have any impact on the relationship between industry performance pressure and financial fraud, so that H6 was refuted. Compared with historical performance, financing demand has no significant moderating effect on the positive correlation between industry performance pressures and financial fraud, one reason for which may be that industry performance has certain volatility and is affected by external policy environment and macroeconomic situation. When external investors determine whether to invest in enterprises, they mainly refer to the historical performance of enterprises, while industry performance is relatively less important as a decision-making reference. Hence, financing demand has no significant moderating effect on the positive correlation between industry performance pressure and financial fraud.

The results of Model 4 show that the degree of industry competition can promote the positive correlation between enterprise historical performance pressure and financial fraud (beta= 0.445, $P < 0.01$), but it does not play a significant moderating effect of the positive correlation between enterprise performance pressure and financial fraud. Compared with the enterprises with lower degree of industry competition, the greater historical performance pressure the enterprise with higher degree of industry competition is faced with, the more financial fraud it will engage in. Thus, H7 was verified. However, the degree of industry competition exerts no impact on the relationship between industry performance pressure and financial fraud, so that H8 was refuted. A key reason why this hypothesis fails to be verified is that, according to the classical S-C-P (Structure-Conduct-Performance Model), when the industry is highly competitive, the vertical comparison of the enterprise (historical performance) is a more critical index than horizontal comparison (industry performance) in evaluating managers' personal ability and performance, and the board of directors is more inclined to judge managers' personal performance by historical performance (Xia et al., 2013). As a result, for managers, the higher the degree of industry competition is, the more the managers will be driven by the historical performance pressure to engage in financial fraud, while they are less driven by the industry performance pressure.

The results of Model 5 show that institutional environment in the region where the firm is located will not only weaken the positive correlation between historical performance pressure and financial fraud (beta=-0.014, $P < 0.001$), but also weaken the positive correlation between industrial performance pressure and financial fraud (beta=-0.063, $P < 0.001$). Compared with the poor institutional environment in the area where the enterprise is located, the better the institutional environment in the area where the enterprise is located is, the lower financial fraud it will engage in with the increase of historical performance pressure and industrial performance pressure. Hence, H9 and H10 were verified. All the above supported results are supported in Model 6 as a full model, and the refuted results are not supported in Model 6.

Table 5-6 Moderating Effect Test between Corporate Performance Pressure and Financial Fraud (N=6,903)

Variables	*FR*					
	M1	M2	M3	M4	M5	M6
HP×PL		0.063***				0.069***
		(0.022)				(0.025)
IP×PL		0.095**				0.115**
		(0.039)				(0.044)
HP×RZ			0.113***			0.069***
			(0.021)			(0.020)
IP×RZ			0.143			0.088
			(0.175)			(0.139)
HP×JZ				0.445**		0.239**
				(0.158)		(0.072)
IP×JZ				0.116		0.095
				(0.104)		(0.089)
HP×IN					-0.014***	-0.015**
					(0.001)	(0.001)
IP×IN					-0.063***	-0.038**
					(0.015)	(0.012)
NL	0.186***	0.178***	0.171***	0.183***	0.179***	0.177***
	(0.033)	(0.041)	(0.038)	(0.050)	(0.040)	(0.039)
GM	0.015	0.187***	0.186***	0.0172	0.008	0.006
	(0.019)	(0.030)	(0.029)	(0.017)	(0.009)	(0.009)
GQ	-0.001	-0.000	-0.000	-0.000	-0.000	-0.000
	(0.000)	(0.000)	(0.000)	(0.000)	(0.000)	(0.000)
RY	-0.032***	-0.024***	-0.024***	-0.024***	-0.018***	-0.019***
	(0.007)	(0.005)	(0.005)	(0.005)	(0.001)	(0.001)
LZ	0.017***	0.033***	0.018***	0.018***	0.710**	-0.155
	(0.004)	(0.009)	(0.005)	(0.005)	(0.347)	(0.217)

Variables	*FR*					
	M1	M2	M3	M4	M5	M6
DD	0.118***	0.015*	0.012*	0.012*	0.012*	0.017**
	(0.032)	(0.006)	(0.005)	(0.005)	(0.005)	(0.006)
GG	0.032+	0.005	0.089*	0.090*	0.090*	0.041
	(0.018)	(0.008)	(0.044)	(0.044)	(0.044)	(0.027)
PL	0.011**	0.053***	0.054***	0.010**	0.029***	0.024***
	(0.004)	(0.008)	(0.008)	(0.004)	(0.006)	(0.006)
RZ	0.016***	0.004**	0.004**	0.016***	0.710**	0.155
	(0.003)	(0.002)	(0.002)	(0.003)	(0.347)	(0.217)
JZ	0.353	-0.133	-0.117	0.406	0.051	0.038
	(0.294)	(0.180)	(0.186)	(0.272)	(0.087)	(0.061)
IN	-0.336***	-0.0223	-0.091**	-0.230***	-0.034*	-0.037*
	(0.042)	(0.074)	(0.043)	(0.088)	(0.019)	(0.020)
HP	0.139***	0.466***	0.424***	0.165***	0.173***	0.289***
	(0.040)	(0.113)	(0.109)	(0.045)	(0.062)	(0.083)
IP	0.162**	0.158**	0.150**	0.169*	0.144**	0.106**
	(0.058)	(0.054)	(0.051)	(0.072)	(0.042)	(0.031)
_Cons	0.951***	0.957***	0.611***	0.607***	0.610***	0.521***
	(0.138)	(0.133)	(0.096)	(0.095)	(0.095)	(0.067)
IND	Control	Control	Control	Control	Control	Control
NF	Control	Control	Control	Control	Control	Control
F	430.541***	334.036***	70.453***	302.479***	168.782***	450.23***
Adj_R^2	0.023	0.025	0.024	0.025	0.025	0.026
N	6903	6903	6903	6903	6903	6903

Notes: $^{+}$P<0.1, *P<0.05, **P<0.01, ***P<0.001, the values in brackets are adjusted standard errors.

In order to further understand the above two interaction effects, this book adopted the method proposed by Aiken & West (1991) to conduct a simple slope test and draw two-dimensional interaction graphs. The interaction graphs in Figure 5-1 and Figure 5-2 show that with the increase of enterprise historical performance pressure and industry performance pressure, enterprises with political connection engage in financial fraud more than those without political connection. The graph in Figure 5-3 shows that with the increase of enterprise historical performance pressure, enterprises with higher financing demand engage in financial fraud more than those with lower financing demand. The graph in Figure 5-4 with the increase of enterprise historical performance pressure, enterprises with higher degree of industry competition engage in financial fraud more than those with lower degree of industry competition. The graphs in Figure 5-5 and Figure 5-6 show that with the increase of enterprise historical performance pressures and industry performance pressures, the enterprise with better institutional environment in the area where the enterprise is located engages less in financial fraud compared with those with poorer institutional environment where they are located.

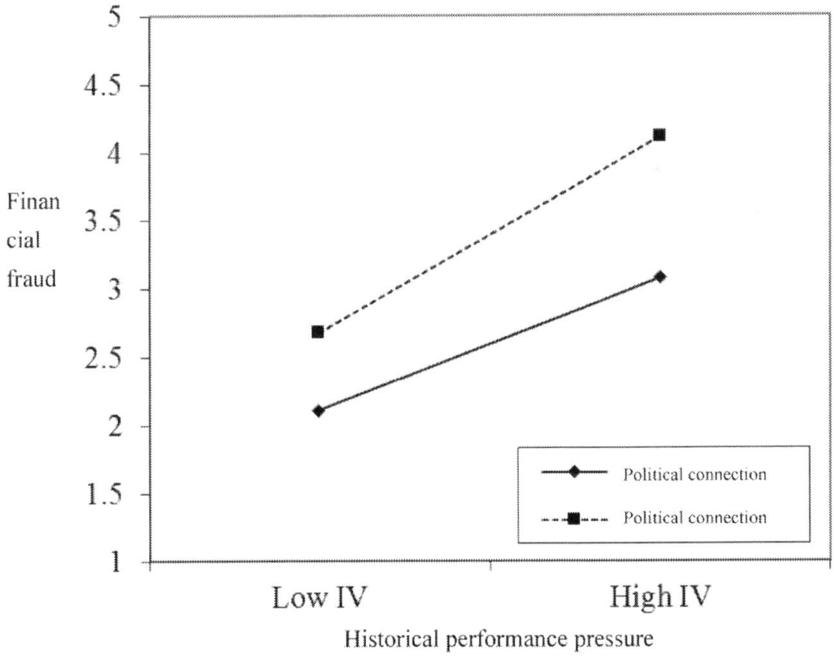

Figure 5-1 Moderating Effect of Political Connection on the Relationship between Historical Performance Pressure and Financial Fraud

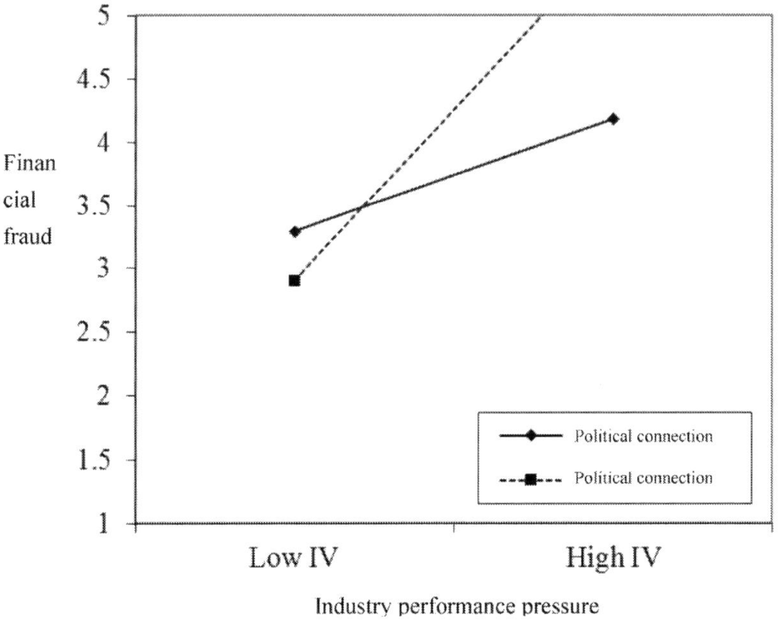

Figure 5-2 Moderating Effect of Political Connection on the Relationship between Industry Performance Pressure and Financial Fraud

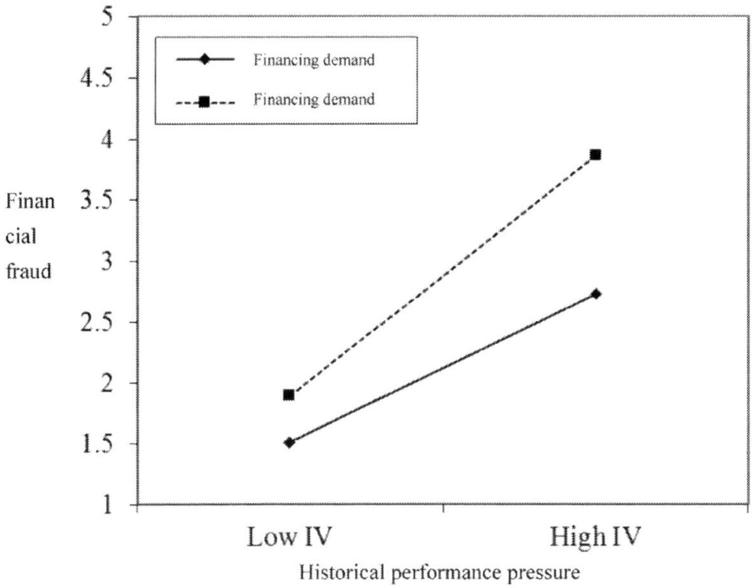

Figure 5-3 Moderating Effect of Financing Demand on the Relationship between Historical Performance Pressure and Financial Fraud

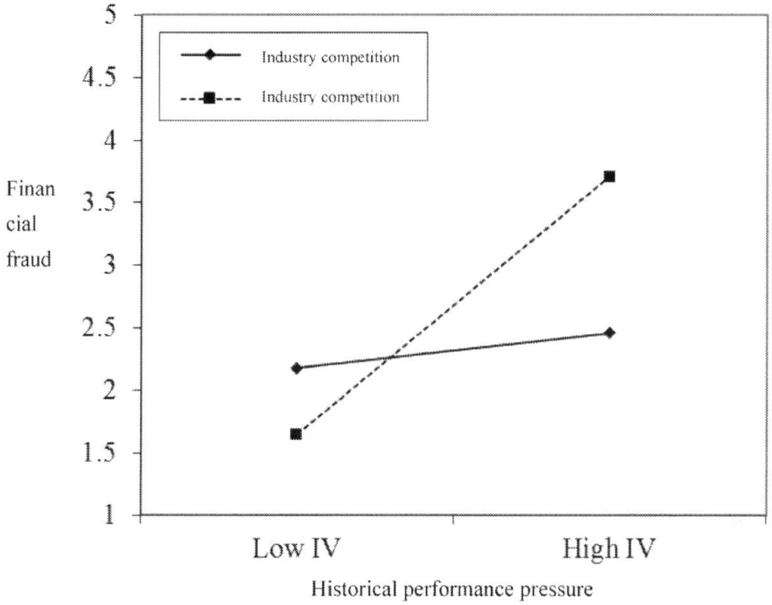

Figure 5-4 Moderating Effect of the Degree of Industry Competition on the Relationship between Historical Performance Pressure and Financial Fraud

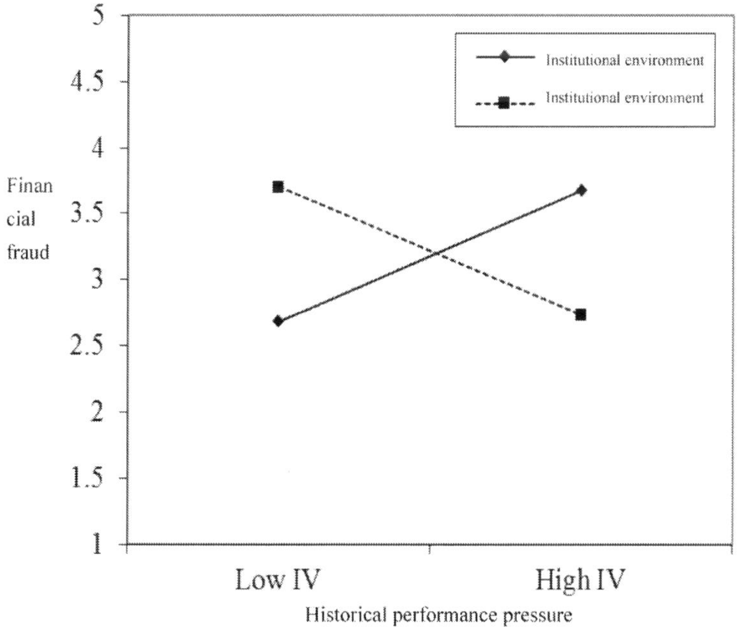

Figure 5-5 Moderating Effect of the Institutional Environment on the Relationship between Historical Performance Pressure and Financial Fraud

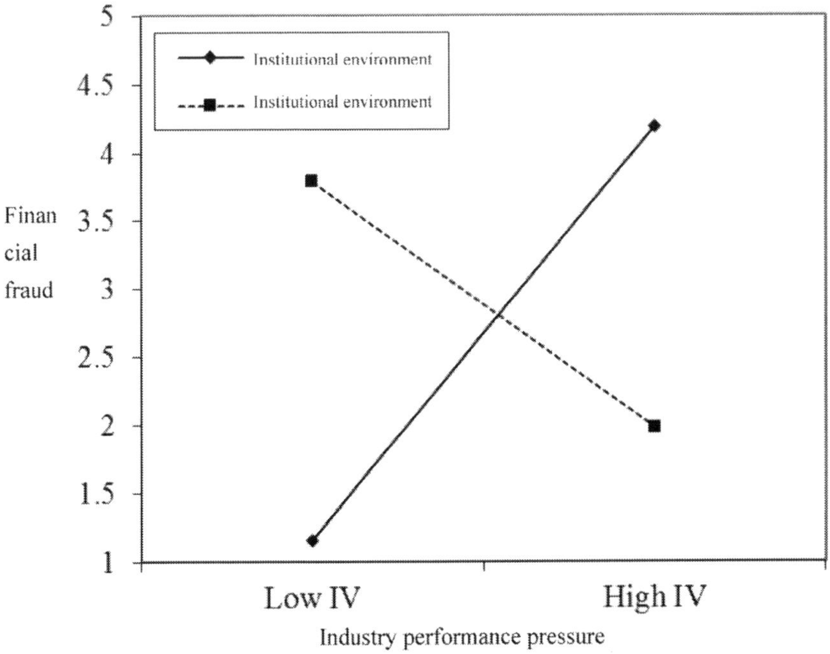

Figure 5-6 Moderating Effect of the Institutional Environment on the Relationship between Industry Performance Pressure and Financial Fraud

Robustness Test

Robustness Test of Substitution Variables of Financial Fraud

In the process of robustness test, firstly, the substitution variables of financial fraud were used to test robustness, and the variables with financial fraud are assigned to 1, otherwise the value is 0. The Logit regression analysis was carried out. The results of robustness test are shown in Table 5-7. The results of Model 1 show that there is a significant positive correlation between enterprise historical performance pressure, industry performance pressure and financial fraud (beta = 1.392, $P < 0.001$; beta = 0.433, $P < 0.001$), and thus H1 and H2 were verified. The results of Model 2 show that political connection can promote the positive correlation between historical performance pressure and financial fraud (beta= 0.432, $P < 0.001$), and also promote the positive correlation between industry performance pressure and financial fraud (beta= 0.059, $P < 0.01$). Compared with the enterprises without political connection, the higher the degree of historical performance pressure and industry performance pressure is in the enterprise with political connection, the more financial fraud it will engage in. Thus, H3 and H4 were verified. For the same reason, H5, H7, H9 and H10 were also verified, but H6 and H8 were not.

Table 5-7 Robustness Test of the Relationship between Performance Pressure and Financial Fraud

Variables	*FR*				
	M1	**M2**	**M3**	**M4**	**M5**
Other variables	*Control*	*Control*	*Control*	*Control*	*Control*
HP	1.392***	1.435***	1.320***	1.355***	1.584***
	(0.310)	(0.312)	(0.321)	(0.322)	(0.589)
IP	0.433***	0.430***	0.421***	0.423***	0.098
	(0.060)	(0.061)	(0.065)	(0.065)	(0.102)
HP×PL		0.432***			
		(0.060)			
IP×PL		0.059***			
		(0.012)			
HP×RZ			0.584**		
			(0.264)		
IP×RZ			0.052		
			(0.104)		
HP×JZ				0.608**	
				(0.262)	
IP×JZ				0.0483	
				(0.105)	
HP×IN					-0.423***
					(0.065)
IP×IN					-0.055***
					(0.013)
_Cons	-6.245***	-6.530***	-8.272***	-8.539***	-7.723***
	(0.570)	(0.585)	(0.654)	(0.674)	(1.263)
IND	*Control*	*Control*	*Control*	*Control*	*Control*

Variables	*FR*				
	M1	**M2**	**M3**	**M4**	**M5**
NF	*Control*	*Control*	*Control*	*Control*	*Control*
Pseudo R^2	0.208	0.212	0.321	0.324	0.353
Chi^2	305.05***	311.09***	469.41***	473.03***	194.03***
N	6903	6903	6903	6903	6903

Notes: +P<0.1, *P<0.05, **P<0.01, ***P<0.001, the values in brackets are adjusted standard errors.

Robustness Test of Substitution Variables of Institutional Environment

Institutional environment, as an important moderating variable in this study, is also a widely representative research scenario in transitional economy. In order to ensure the robustness of the results, the author used the substitution variables of institutional environment to test the robustness of the regression results. For substitution variables of institutional environment, the World Bank's report on China Governance, Investment Climate, and Harmonious Society: Competitiveness Enhancements for 120 Cities in China, published in 2006, was adopted for testing. In order to facilitate the world to understand the differences of investment environment in different regions of China, the Asian Department of the World Bank organized a large-scale survey report on the investment environment of Chinese cities in 2005, which covered 120 cities in Southeast China, the Bohai Rim Region, Central China, Northeast China, Southwest China and Northwest China. Among them, 200 enterprises were selected from Beijing, Shanghai, Tianjin and Chongqing municipalities directly under the Central Government, and 100 enterprises were selected from other cities, while a total of more than 12,400 enterprises were sampled, including state-owned enterprises, private enterprises and foreign-funded enterprises, accounting for 8%, 64% and 28% respectively (World Bank Report, 2006). The World Bank's institutional environment index for 120 cities in mainland China is shown in Table 5-8②.

② There are mainly the following methods to measure the overall institutional environment. Firstly, it is the marketization index, which is mostly used in existing

In the process of robustness test, this study re-ranked the institutional development of different regions in China according to the World Bank Report 2006. According to the division of Southeast China, the Bohai Rim Region, Central China, Northeast China, Southwest China, and Northwest China, the mean value of institutional environment index of cities in each region was calculated, which represents the institutional environment index of the region, and then the hypotheses were re-tested. The results of Model 1 show that there is a significant positive correlation between enterprise historical performance pressure, industry performance pressures and financial fraud (beta = 0.137, $P < 0.001$; beta = 0.159, $P < 0.001$). Thus, H1 and H2 were verified. The results of Model 4 show that regional institutional environment will not only weaken the positive correlation between historical performance pressure and financial fraud (beta=-0.078, $P < 0.01$), but also weaken the positive correlation between industry performance pressure and financial fraud (beta=-0.120, $P < 0.01$). Compared with the enterprises without political connection, the greater historical performance pressure and industry performance pressure the enterprise with political connection is faced with, the more financial fraud it will engage in. Thus, H9 and H10 were verified. For the same reason, H2, H3, H5 and H7 were also verified, but H6 and H8 were not.

---

studies to measure the institutional environment of different regions, as there is often better institutional environment in the areas which are highly marketized as a whole. Secondly, it is the sub-index of the marketization index. Gao et al. measured the institutional environment of different regions with the sub-indexes of marketization index, namely, the development of market intermediary organizations and legal institutional environment and the development degree of product market. Ding Lieyun and Liu Rongying used the sub-index of the development degree of factor market to measure the institutional environment of different regions. Thirdly, it is the GDP and government budget. One of the important purposes of China's institutional transformation is to establish a sound market economic system, where the resources are allocated more by market than by government, compared with planned economy. The more thorough the institutional transition is, the greater role the market will play in the allocation of resources. In this regard, some studies measure the institutional environment with the help of the role of market in the allocation of resources. Fourthly, there are other ways. Based on the survey data, Jiang Chunyan and Zhao Shuming measured the institutional environment of entrepreneurship in various regions, focusing on reflecting the degree of support of institutional environment for entrepreneurship and innovation activities. One of the main reasons why the data of the World Bank is used for robustness test in this study is that the marketization index of the World Bank is more authoritative than other ways.

Table 5-8 Property Rights Protection Index of Major Cities in China

City	Score	City	Score	City	Score	City	Score	City	Score	City	Score
Hangzhou	0.982	Jinzhou	0.786	Guilin	0.724	Changzhou	0.661	Jingzhou	0.552	Kunming	0.435
Shantou	0.960	Sanming	0.794	Baoding	0.713	Jinhua	0.658	Hefei	0.542	Zunyi	0.430
Qingdao	0.950	Shijiazhuang	0.793	Linyi	0.709	Changsha	0.651	Qiqihar	0.539	Baotou	0.418
Shangrao	0.946	Xiaogan	0.793	Maoming	0.706	Dalian	0.649	Shenyang	0.543	Xi'an	0.420
Jiangmen	0.936	Chuzhou	0.780	Chongqing	0.709	Jilin	0.655	Yancheng	0.535	Changde	0.411
Suzhou	0.934	Quanzhou	0.777	Changchun	0.697	Qujing	0.654	Foshan	0.528	Handan	0.408
Zhoukou	0.926	Shaoxing	0.781	Huanggang	0.700	Huzhou	0.630	Yinchuan	0.529	Fushun	0.398
Jiujiang	0.882	Tai'an	0.404	Jingmen	0.703	Wuhu	0.825	Tangshan	0.522	Taizhou	0.688
Shangqiu	0.868	Yuncheng	0.768	Leshan	0.700	Nanjing	0.617	Xianyang	0.506	Xiangfan	0.396
Zibo	0.864	Fuzhou	0.758	Lianyungang	0.696	Yueyang	0.616	Harbin	0.498	Xinxiang	0.402
Jining	0.849	Ningbo	0.758	Yangzhou	0.698	Baoji	0.612	Urumqi	0.496	Dongguan	0.387
Yichang	0.835	Huizhou	0.753	Yichun	0.702	Guangzhou	0.612	Luoyang	0.484	Hengyang	0.389
Deyang	0.833	Nanchang	0.750	Mianyang	0.687	Tianjin	0.611	Wuxi	0.482	Wuhan	0.630
Weihai	0.826	Nantong	0.746	Taiyuan	0.782	Xuzhou	0.610	Cangzhou	0.466	Lanzhou	0.377
Wuzhong	0.391	Weifang	0.751	Zhangzhou	0.690	Xuchang	0.569	Guiyang	0.471	Daqing	0.369
Xiamen	0.832	Zhengzhou	0.746	Qinghuangdao	0.683	Ganzhou	0.558	Haikou	0.475	Nanning	0.357
Yantai	0.832	Langfang	0.741	Zhuhai	0.683	Ji'nan	0.561	Shanghai	0.449	Xining	0.356
Anqing	0.809	Shenzhen	0.740	Anshan	0.673	Nanyang	0.562	Tianshui	0.447	Zhuzhou	0.361
Chenzhou	0.809	Yuxi	0.728	Liuzhou	0.675	Yibin	0.560	Wenzhou	0.443	Datong	0.296
Jiaxing	0.790	Chengdu	0.724	Zhangjiakou	0.674	Benxi	0.548	Beijing	0.429	Hohhot	0.269

Data source: World Bank. 2006. China Governance, Investment Climate, and Harmonious Society: Competitiveness Enhancements for 120 Cities in China (Report Number: 37759-CN)

Table 5-9 Robustness Test of the Relationship between Performance Pressure and Financial Fraud

Variables	***FR*** M1	M2	M3	M4	M5	M6
Other variables	*Control*	*Control*	*Control*	*Control*	*Control*	*Other variables*
HP	0.137***	0.466***	0.424***	0.165***	0.173***	0.289***
	(0.040)	(0.113)	(0.109)	(0.045)	(0.062)	(0.083)
IP	0.159**	0.158**	0.150**	0.169*	0.144**	0.106**
	(0.058)	(0.054)	(0.051)	(0.072)	(0.042)	(0.031)
HP×PL		**0.063*** **				0.069***
		(0.022)				(0.025)
IP×PL		**0.095** **				0.115**
		(0.039)				(0.044)
HP×RZ			**0.113*** **			0.069***
			(0.021)			(0.020)
IP×RZ			0.143			0.088
			(0.175)			(0.139)
HP×JZ				**0.445** **		0.239**
				(0.158)		(0.072)
IP×JZ				0.116		0.095
				(0.104)		(0.089)
HP×IN					**-0.078** **	-0.064**
					(0.021)	(0.019)
IP×IN					**-0.102** **	-0.106*
					(0.034)	(0.038)
_Cons	0.951***	0.944***	0.592***	0.591***	0.592***	0.873***
	(0.138)	(0.130)	(0.096)	(0.095)	(0.095)	(0.138)
IND	*Control*	*Control*	*Control*	*Control*	*Control*	*Control*
NF	*Control*	*Control*	*Control*	*Control*	*Control*	*Control*
F	430.541***	559.134***	69.803***	461.058***	253.400***	388.609****
Adj_R²	0.023	0.025	0.023	0.024	0.024	0.024
N	5488	5488	5488	5488	5488	5488

Notes: $^{+}$P<0.1, *P<0.05, **P<0.01, ***P<0.001, the values in brackets are adjusted standard errors.

Further Analysis

Impact of Financial Fraud on Corporate risk

Through the above empirical analysis, it can be found that, based on the analysis framework of prospect theory, business managers, as a rational decision maker with personal income as the fundamental decision-making point, will choose financial fraud to avoid the short-term loss of personal benefits in the face of the historical performance pressures and industry performance pressures of the enterprise, while the external industry factors and institutional factors will further affect the decision-making of individuals. However, from the perspective of the reversal effect of reference point in prospect theory, do managers make the decision because they have anticipated that financial fraud will not increase the risk of the enterprise? That is to say, in the current situation of China, can financial fraud really increase the risk of enterprises for managers? The author constructed the following research model for testing:

$$RSK_{i,t} = \beta_0 + \beta_1 FR_{i,t} + \sum_{i=1}^{n} \alpha_i \times Control_i + \delta \quad (1)$$

In the formula, $RSK_{i,t}$ represents corporate risk, $FR_{i,t}$ represents the financial fraud of the enterprise and $Control_i$ represents all control variables, including enterprise age(NL), enterprise scale(GM), ownership concentration(GQ), organizational slack(RY), separation of chairman and CEO(LZ), ratio of independent directors(DD), shareholding ratio of senior executives(CG), annual dummy variables(NF), and industry dummy variable. δ represents the residual.

At present, the main indicators to measure corporate risk in the literature are volatility of earnings (John et al., 2008; Yu et al., 2013), debt ratio (Faccio et al., 2011), and annual beta coefficient (Montgomery & Singh, 1984; Barton, 1988; Zhang & Huang, 2009), among which the first two are generally used to measure the long-term corporate risk during the rolling period of three to five years. It is not consistent with the corporate risk in the same year that should be studied in this book. Therefore, this book used the annual beta coefficient to measure the corporate risk, which was directly taken from the CSMAR database to measure the market risk faced by the enterprise in that year from the perspective of investors in a more objective way. The regression results of the fixed effects model show that financial fraud will increase the risk of enterprises, which further demonstrates that managers tend to be self-interested when they engage in financial fraud, so that they choose to ignore the long-term benefits of enterprises mainly from the perspective of short-term benefits of individuals. Jiang et al. (2018) has also found in the recent research that the managers are replaced more frequently in the companies that engage in financial fraud.

Table 5-10 Relational Test between Financial Fraud and Corporate Risk

Variables	***RSK***	
	M1	**M2**
FR		**0.213***
		(0.082)
PL	0.023	0.028
	(0.020)	(0.022)
RZ	0.027+	0.153***
	(0.014)	(0.045)
JZ	0.036***	0.030***
	(0.008)	(0.009)
IN	0.042	0.048
	(0.026)	(0.028)
Other variables	Control	Control
IND	Control	Control
NF	Control	Control
F	258.152***	158.262***
Adj_R^2	0.030	0.041
N	6903	6903

Notes: $^{+}$P<0.1, *P<0.05, **P<0.01, ***P<0.001, the values in brackets are adjusted standard errors.

Impact of Financial Fraud on Corporate Performance

From the above test, it can be found that with the gradual deepening of China's market-oriented reform and the continuous improvement of the market system, financial fraud of managers will significantly increase the risk of enterprises. So in the long run, will the enterprises that are disclosed to the public of the engagement in financial fraud have poorer performance when such financial fraud is discovered? The author constructed the following model for testing:

$$PRO_{i,t} = \beta_0 + \beta_1 CFR_{i,t} + \sum_{i=1}^{n} \alpha_i \times Control_i + \delta \quad (1)$$

In the formula, $PRO_{i,t}$ represents corporate performance, $CFR_{i,t}$ represents the the number of times an enterprise has been detected for financial fraud and $Control_i$ represents all control variables, including enterprise age(NL), enterprise scale(GM), ownership concentration(GQ), organizational slack(RY), separation of chairman and CEO(LZ), ratio of independent directors(DD), shareholding ratio of senior executives(CG), annual dummy variables(NF), and industry dummy variable. δ represents the residual.

This model mainly detects the impact of the number of financial frauds of an enterprise that have been investigated by China Securities Regulatory Commission on corporate performance at the cut-off point of the time t, while the potential fraudulent acts can not be excluded. The performance of enterprises is mainly measured by two indexes, annual stock return of individual stock (SR) and ROA [log (1 + ROA)]. As shown in Table 5-11, according to the results of the next year (t=1), the next two years (t=2) and the next three years (t=3), financial fraud of an enterprise has always had a significant negative impact on its stock return, which, to a certain extent, confirms the traditional signaling theory that an enterprise will be always accompanied by its financial fraud as a stigma and that investors in the market will consciously and automatically select companies with the records of financial fraud, when they choose to invest in stocks, thereby leading to a continuous decline in the stock returns of such companies. In contrast, financial fraud and corporate ROA have significant negative effects in the short term (t = 1, t = 2), but in the long run, the negative effects will gradually weaken, for which there may be two reasons. On the one hand, in the short term, financial fraud of an enterprise may pose a serious impact on its reputation in the market, impair the trust between potential stakeholders of the enterprise, and increase the transaction costs between the enterprise and its consumers, suppliers and partners in the upstream and downstream industrial chains, thus impairing the short-term performance of the enterprise. But in the long run, with the long-term contacts and repeated games between enterprises and their potential stakeholders, they will build trust in each other again, which will gradually eliminate the negative impact of the financial fraud scandal. A typical example in China's A-share market is the Shuanghui Case. On the other hand, when a financial fraud scandal breaks out in an enterprise, there tends to be frequent turnover in the management in general, and the managerial staff, who are either promoted from the internal candidates or parachuted from outsiders, need to adapt to the environment of the enterprise and implement strategic decisions in a transition period. The cost of coordination in the early stage will also reduce the performance of enterprises, but in the long run, such cost will gradually decrease.

Table 5-11 Relational Test between Financial Fraud and Corporate Performance

Variables	***SR*(t=1)**		***SR*(t=2)**	***SR*(t=3)**	***ROA*(t=1)**		***ROA*(t=2)**	***ROA*(t=3)**
	M1	M2	M3	M4	M5	M6	M7	M8
FR		**-0.09⁺**	**-0.04****	**-0.05****		**-0.05****	**-0.12****	-0.22
		(0.04)	**(0.02)**	**(0.02)**		**(0.02)**	**(0.06)**	(0.23)
PL	0.15	0.15	0.17**	0.16**	0.14⁺	0.13⁺	0.01	0.02**
	(0.11)	(0.11)	(0.08)	(0.08)	(0.08)	(0.08)	(0.01)	(0.01)
RZ	-0.29	-0.27	-0.14	-0.18	-0.04	-0.06	1.58***	1.42***
	(0.43)	(0.43)	(0.36)	(0.37)	(0.24)	(0.24)	(0.58)	(0.41)
JZ	0.64**	0.63**	-0.00	-0.00	-0.14	-0.17	-0.19	0.000
	(0.30)	(0.30)	(0.00)	(0.00)	(0.24)	(0.25)	(0.81)	(0.40)
IN	-0.28	-0.27	-0.09	-0.13	0.01	0.01	-1.52***	-1.28*
	(0.25)	(0.25)	(0.23)	(0.24)	(0.04)	(0.04)	(0.54)	(0.76)
Other variables	*Control*	*Control*	*Control*	*Control*	*Control*	*Control*	*Control*	*Control*
IND	*Control*	*Control*	*Control*	*Control*	*Control*	*Control*	*Control*	*Control*
NF	*Control*	*Control*	*Control*	*Control*	*Control*	*Control*	*Control*	*Control*
Adj_R^2	0.049	0.063	0.092	0.103	0.046	0.087	0.105	0.063
N	1105	1105	785	594	1105	1105	785	594

Notes: ⁺P<0.1, *P<0.05, **P<0.01, ***P<0.001, the values in brackets are adjusted standard errors.

Summary of Hypothesis Tests

This chapter makes regression analysis of the above-mentioned hypotheses. First of all, the main effects and the impacts of historical performance pressures and industry performance pressures on financial fraud were tested. Secondly, the moderating effects of corporate political connection, financing demand, the degree of industry competition and regional institutional environment on the main effect were tested from the individual level, the organizational level and the regional environment level. In the process of testing the above hypotheses, the author mainly chose the sample data of listed companies after the revised Accounting Standards in 2007. The samples were mainly concentrated in the listed companies in the Shanghai and Shenzhen A-share markets in China from 2007 to 2015, and the above hypotheses were tested by the fixed effects model of panel data. The main test results are shown in Table 5-11.

Table 5-11 Summary of Results of Hypothesis Tests

Research hypothesis	**Test result**
H1: With the increase of enterprises' historical performance pressures, enterprises will adopt higher illegal financial frauds.	**Support**
H2: With the increase of enterprises' industry performance pressures, enterprises will adopt higher illegal financial frauds.	**Support**
H3: Compared with the enterprises without political connections, enterprises with the background of government relations are more likely to engage in illegal financial fraud with the increase of historical performance pressure.	**Support**
H4: Compared with the enterprises without political connections, enterprises with the background of government relations are more likely to engage in illegal financial fraud with the increase of industry performance pressure.	**Support**
H5: Compared with the enterprises with lower financing demand, the higher the financing demand of the company is, the greater illegal financial fraud the company will engage in with the increase in its historical performance pressure.	**Support**

Research hypothesis	Test result
H6: Compared with the enterprises with lower financing demand, the higher the financing demand of the company is, the greater illegal financial fraud the company will engage in with the increase in its industry performance pressure.	**Refute**
H7: Compared with the enterprises which are located in less competitive industries, the fiercer the competition in the industry where the company is located is, the greater illegal financial fraud the company will engage in with the increase in its historical performance pressure.	**Support**
H8: Compared with the enterprises which are located in less competitive industries, the fiercer the competition in the industry where the company is located is, the greater illegal financial fraud the company will engage in with the increase in its industry performance pressure.	**Refute**
H9: The better the institutional environment in the area where the enterprise is located is, the lower the degree of illegal financial fraud adopted by the enterprise will be with the increase of its historical performance pressures.	**Support**
H10: The better the institutional environment in the area where the enterprise is located is, the lower the degree of illegal financial fraud adopted by the enterprise will be with the increase of its industry performance pressures.	**Support**

Chapter 6 Research Conclusions and Prospects

Major Research Conclusions

Corporate strategic decision-making is a fundamental decision-making on the direction of development. However, in the practices of business management in China, the frequent errors in business strategy remind us that the quality of strategic decision-making needs to be further improved. The mechanism of corporate strategic decision-making involves a complex and dynamic process, which is closely related to a large number of factors inside and outside the organization and faced with information collection, information abandonment, search cost, uncertainty, ambiguity and various conflicts. As far as managers are concerned, the strategic choice under corporate performance pressure is the key for enterprises to make decisions on behavior, which directly determines whether the enterprise can be reborn. This issue is also one of the focuses of the practice and academic circles. Manager is the direct maker of corporate strategic decision, which is the direct embodiment of managers' personal values to a certain extent. However, in the transitional period of China, managers are more likely to make a reckless move to engage in financial fraud under performance pressure due to the less perfect markets and institutions. The existing research on financial fraud is mainly based on the cost-benefit analysis from a single perspective, which directly results in the lack of explanatory power of the existing research conclusions. Based on prospect theory and institutional theory, this study examines the action mechanism and influence mechanism between performance pressure and financial fraud of listed companies in China. Especially from the perspective of institutional theory, it discusses the impact of the unique institutional environment on the relationship between performance pressure and financial fraud in the transition period of China. Based on the samples of 6,903 listed companies in the Shanghai and Shenzhen stock exchanges from 2007 to 2015, the following conclusions are drawn based on the regression analysis of the fixed effects model of panel data.

Corporate performance pressure is a key driving force leading to financial fraud.

Separation of ownership and control in the modern corporate governance model directly leads to the quantified performance indicators as the only criteria for assessing managers' competence. In terms of managers, corporate performance not only directly affects the actual income of individuals, but also determines the position of individuals in the company and their reputation in the job market. As a result, managers tend to show more short-sighted egoism than corporate owners. When the performance of the company is lower than historical expected performance and industry expected performance, managers, as the main decision makers of strategies, often choose to engage in financial fraud for the sake of personal interests, and whitewash their financial performance so as to achieve the purpose of improving the performance of the enterprise, alleviating its performance pressure and thus increasing personal earnings. Although it is not excluded that managers will improve the performance of enterprises through positive strategic changes in the face of performance pressures, short-sighted managers tend to choose the financial fraud with little investment but quick result due to the driving force of quick win so as to ease performance pressure and increase personal earnings, compared with the costs and cycles necessary for such positive strategic changes as innovation investment.

The political connection asylum arising from the unique institutional environment in the transition period will further motivate enterprises to engage in financial fraud.

In the transition period, China's market economy has made great progress, but the construction of political and legal systems has failed to keep pace with the pace of economic development, and enterprises are less protected by formal systems in the operating process. Lack of formal systems, such as backward financial system, excessive government intervention, and severe non-tax burden, has led the enterprises to seek political connection to replace formal systems. In the economic environment where the system is less perfect, political connection has benefited the private enterprises in various aspects, including financing facilities, tax incentives, and preferential government assistance in times of financial crisis. However, political connection is also a double-edged sword. However, political connection is also a double-edged sword. While giving enterprises competitive edges, political connection also facilitates the management with political connection to infringe on investors' interests based on its power in hand, which may be either manifested as the directors representing the interests of the government forcing enterprises to achieve the political goals of the government, or as the substantial shareholders with political connections infringing on the interests of minority shareholders. For business managers, the umbrella formed by political connection may enhance their financial fraud under performance pressure. On the one hand, the enterprises with political connection have higher legitimacy when engaging in financial fraud, which can reduce the supervision cost of financial fraud. On the other hand, the asylum of political connection also allows managers to avoid the penalty costs for financial fraud afterwards. As a result, when the managers are politically connected, they are more inclined to financial fraud under the pressure of historical expected performance and industry expected performance.

The abundance of organizational resources and the industry competition are important boundary conditions to promote or restrain financial fraud.

Pfeffer & Salancik (1978) systematically elaborated the theory of resource dependence in the book The External Control of Organizations: A Resource Dependence Perspective, which holds that when the actor is unable to completely control the conditions of taking an action or achieving a result, he or she will become dependent on the external environment. Since the behavior of an organization is influenced by the surrounding organizations and environment, the organization will depend on the resources of the environment, and respond to the uncertainty of resources. As an open form of organization, the enterprise has exchanged its resources with its stakeholders in the external environment, which determines its dependence on external resources, while such dependence is closely bound up with the ownership of its resources and the degree of industry competition. In terms of managers, corporate performance pressures will directly affect their personal income and lead them to engage in financial fraud, while the degree of redundancy of resources and the degree of industry competition are also the key factors affecting their decision-making. In case that an enterprise has a lack of resources and is heavily dependent on external resources with a higher financing demand, corporate performance, as a direct signal, will directly determine whether it can get the support of external funds. In this case, the historical performance pressure (vertical comparison) of enterprises is the key to determine the support of resources from their stakeholders, while managers will tend more to commit financial fraud in order to maintain the stable resource demand of enterprises. In the meantime, when the industry is in a state of increasingly intense competition, managers may improve the performance of enterprises by whitewashing financial statements and alleviate the historical performance pressure so as to cope with the competitive strategy of competitors in the industry market, which is the key to avoid loss of personal earnings and dismission. Hence, the results show that both financing demand and the degree of industry competition of enterprises may enhance the positive correlation between historical expected performance pressure and financial fraud, while they fail to play a significant role in moderating the relationship between industry expected performance pressure and financial fraud.

Regional institutional environment is an important institutional factor that restricts corporate financial fraud.

At present, the mainstream theory of corporate strategic management can be divided into two perspectives in research. One is the industry-based view represented by Porter (1980), which holds that industrial factors determine the strategy and performance of enterprises to the greatest extent, and the other is the resource-based view, represented by Barney (1991), which emphasizes that different characteristics of an enterprise determine its strategy and performance. In fact, these two views neglect the institutional factors that are in favor of industrial competition or business characteristics playing a role, and regard the free market economy and democratic political system as the background. Recently, the studies by scholars on China and other transition economies have shown that the interaction between formal or informal systems, known as game rules, and organizations such as enterprises, has a significant impact on the formation of strategies and changes in performance. As a result, such institution-based view is regarded as a new starting point to explain the strategic choice of enterprises in countries with economies in transition.

North (1990) and other scholars, on the basis of the original theory, believe that enterprises should not only analyze the characteristics of industrial organization and the status of enterprise resources, but also take into account the impact of social system factors in different countries and regions on enterprise behavior. Moreover, they have analyzed it from sociological perspectives, such as local factors and cultural factors, as well as from the perspective of institutional theory, such as formal and informal systems. The institution-based view mainly lays stress on the important role of legitimacy mechanism in organizational structure and interaction between organizations and institutional environment in explaining the strategic behavior of enterprises. As far as managers of enterprises in transition are concerned, external institutional environment is the key factor affecting the strategic choices of their enterprises. In case of more perfect external institutional environment and performance pressure, managers will tend less to choose financial fraud. On the one hand, a perfect institutional environment reduces the possibility of financial fraud, while on the other hand, such environment may increase the penalty cost of financial fraud.

Research Contributions and Innovations

This study attempts to expand and enrich previous studies from the following perspectives:

First of all, based on the prospect theory, the venture speculation strategy of enterprises is incorporated into the performance pressure-strategic choice analysis framework, which extends the boundaries of the existing research on the strategic choice of enterprises. The theory of the firm proposed by Baumol (1990) emphasizes that in addition to legitimate business activities, enterprises may also choose to engage in unproductive and destructive activities (Friedman et al., 2003). However, the existing research mainly focuses on the positive and legitimate strategic behavior of enterprises, and selectively ignores the exploration into the strategic behavior of enterprises violating laws and rules. In this study, the illegal financial frauds of enterprises are incorporated into the analysis framework, which further improves the existing research on prospect theory.

Secondly, the corporate political capital and the macroscopic institutional efficiency at the intermediate level are incorporated into the prospect theory model, which not only enriches the Chinese scenario of this topic and expands the application of institutional theory in the field of corporate strategy research, but also responds to the theoretical logic of the institution-based view for the first time from the perspective of quantitative analysis (Peng, 2008). Peng (2008) proposed the view that the strategic choice of an enterprise depends on the balance of existing external institutional efficiencies, the extent of which determines the cost of strategic choice for the enterprise, and then restricts its business behavior. From the perspective of quantitative analysis, this book gives positive feedback on the application of this theory in the Chinese context.

In terms of practice, this book has the following enlightenments:

1) In the face of external performance pressures, enterprises will choose to engage in financial fraud, one fundamental reason for which is that there are some institutional asylum mechanisms in the context of transition economy in China, which leads to the benefits of financial fraud exceeding the cost to be paid. During the period of transition economy in China, the capital market is lacking in standardized system and effective supervision, while business managers or substantial shareholders can obtain excess profits with the aid of financial fraud. In contrast, financial fraud covers a relatively low cost. It is a necessary way to reduce corporate financial fraud to further deepen the market reform, establish standardized systems and enforce strict supervision.

2) The original intention of entrepreneurs acting as deputies to the NPC and the members of the CPPCC is to commend entrepreneurs for their contribution to regional economic growth. However, it is found in this study that the political capital of enterprises will provide an umbrella for their engagement in financial fraud, and reduce the risk and cost of punishment.

Limitations and Prospects of the Research

Although this book attempts to abide by the scientific and normative research paradigm in the process, it is hard to avoid some limitations and deficiencies due to the complexity of the topic and the limitation of the author's personal ability and energy, which are mainly reflected in the following three aspects:

Firstly, this study attempts to link macro and micro perspectives to analyze the motives and influencing factors of financial fraud by managers, but performance pressure, including historical performance and industry performance, is only one of the important factors that lead managers to choose financial fraud. Managers' engagement in financial fraud is also likely to be closely linked up with their personal experience, personality traits and organizational culture. The latest research on corporate TMT (top management team) has introduced the imprint theory of sociology and found that managers' personal decision-making is closely related to their previous organizational imprints, that their personal preferences for decision-making are the direct manifestation of their organizational imprints, and that their previous military experience and special professional experience are the key factors to personal imprints. The impact of these unique factors on managers' personal decision-making, especially in financial fraud, has been involved in the cutting-edge studies abroad. However, this book just serves as a starting point, and these factors are not only the problems that this book can not solve, but also the direction worth studying in the future. One possible impact of managers' personal organizational imprints on the conclusions of this study is that the conclusions of this study lay stress on the irrational decision-making behavior of managers and attribute irrational decision-making behavior to performance expectation (pressure). In contrast, the organizational imprint perspective attributes managers' decision-making to their individual traits on the premise of emphasizing the irrationality of managers' decision-making. One of the deviations that may be caused by the two different views is that the conclusion of this study emphasizes the commonality of managers (personal homogeneity), while the organizational imprint perspective lays more emphasis on the uniqueness of managers (personal heterogeneity). In this regard, the conclusion of this study may not be applicable in explaining some special manager groups, such as military CEO.

Secondly, prospect theory is the core theory of managers' decision-making on financial fraud that attempts to be expounded in this book, one of the key concepts of which is to emphasize the irrationality of decision makers under varying degrees of risk. The author has always adhered to this fundamental logic in the theoretical deduction of this study, the author is unable to choose the appropriate variables to scale the irrationality of managers; decision-making under varying degrees of risk in the empirical research, which is likely to affect the universality and generalizability of the conclusions of this study. However, it is worth noting that, the future researchers may adopt experimental methods to conduct more in-depth studies on managers' financial fraud by simulating various experimental scenarios, with the rise of experimental research methods (Cheng et al., 2009) in the fields of strategy, corporate governance and entrepreneurship.

Thirdly, performance pressure is introduced as a reference point for enterprise behavior decision-making in this book, but it is really difficult to measure performance pressure directly and adopt indirect criteria commonly adopted by the international academic circles. Even so, it is still possible to be more precise about the choice of reference. In this book, the performance of the enterprise in the previous year and the average performance of the same industry are taken as the reference point, while the concept of reference group proposed by social comparison theory may need to further take into account the several similar characteristics of the object. In addition to industry, such factors as scale, strategy and so on, may be factors worthy of detailed consideration in future research. This study attempts to clearly depict the performance pressure for managers from the vertical dimension of historical performance pressure and the horizontal dimension of industry performance pressure, believing that the performance pressures of these two dimensions are equally important to managers from a subjective point of view. But that may not be the case. Especially for those enterprises which are in the leading position in the industry, the operating situation of enterprises may not be accurately and truly reflected from the industry performance, as they have had no competitors for a long time. In this case, historical performance is a more accurate reference point. As a result, there may be differences in the influence of historical performance pressure and industry performance pressure on managers' decision-making behavior, which may lead to the lack of explanatory power of the conclusions of this study in explaining financial fraud of the oligarch in the industry as a special object.

Bibliography

Adhikari, A., Derashid, C., and Zhang, H. (2006). Public policy, political connections, and effective tax rates: longitudinal evidence from Malaysia. Journal of Accounting & Public Policy, Vol. 25(5): 574-595.

Aguilera, R. V., Desender, K., Bednar, M. K., and Lee, J. H. (2015). Connecting the dots: bringing external corporate governance into the corporate governance puzzle. Academy of Management Annals, Vol. 9(1): 483-573.

Albrecht, C., Holland, D., Malagueño, R., Dolan, S., and Tzafrir, S. (2015). The role of power in fraudulent financial reporting schemes. Journal of Business Ethics, Vol. 131(4): 803-813.

Albrecht W. S., Albrecht C. C., and Albrecht C. O. (2004). "Fraud & Corporate Executives: Agency, Stewardship & Broken Trust", Journal of Forensic Accounting, Vol. 5(1): 109-130.

Apostolou B., Dorminey J. W., Hassell J. M., and Rebele J. E. (2016). "Accounting Education Literature Review (2015)", Journal of Accounting Education, 35, 20-55.

Ashforth, B. E., Gioia, D. A., Robinson, S. L., and Treviño, L. K. (2008). Re-viewing organizational corruption. Academy of Management Review, Vol. 33(3): 670-684.

Audia, P. G., and Greve, H. R. (2006). Less likely to fail: low performance, firm size, and factory expansion in the shipbuilding industry. Management Science, Vol. 52(1): 83-94.

Baginski, S. P., Hassell, J. M., and Kimbrough, M. D. (2002). The effect of legal environment on voluntary disclosure: evidence from management earnings forecasts issued in u.s. and canadian markets. Accounting Review, Vol.77(1): 25-50.

Barberis, N. C. (2013). Thirty years of prospect theory in economics: a review and assessment. Journal of Economic Perspectives, Vol. 27(1): 173-195.

Barkma, H. (2010). Do top managers work harder when they are monitored?. Kyklos, Vol. 48(1): 19-42.

Barr, P. S., and Glynn, M. A. (2004). Cultural variations in strategic issue interpretation: relating cultural uncertainty avoidance to controllability in discriminating threat and opportunity. Strategic Management Journal, Vol.25(1): 59–67.

Baucus M. S. and Near J. P. (1991). Can Illegal Corporate Behavior be Predicted: an Event History Analysis.. Academy of Management Journal, Vol. 34(1): 9-36.

Baum, J. A. C., and Dahlin, K. B. (2007). Aspiration performance and railroads' patterns of learning from train wrecks and crashes. Organization Science, Vol. 18(3): 368-385.

Baumol W. J. (1990). Entrepreneurship: Productive, Unproductive, & Destructive. Journal of Political Economy, Vol. 98(5).

Beasley M. S. (1996). An Empirical Analysis of the Relation Between the Board of Director Composition & Fraudulent financial reporting. Accounting Review, Vol. 71(4): 443-465.

Beasley M. S., and Hermanson D. R. (2006). How Sales Executives Can Avoid Accounting Fraud Allegations. Review of Business, Vol. 27(1): 33-40.

Beasley, M. S., Carcello, J. V., Hermanson, D. R., and Lapides, P. D. (2000). Fraudulent financial reporting: consideration of industry traits and corporate governance mechanisms. Accounting Horizons, Vol. 14(4): 441-454.

Becker G. S. (1976). The Economic Approach to Human Behavior. University of Chicago Press, Chicago, IL.

Bednar, M. K., Boivie, S., and Prince, N. R. (2013). Burr under the saddle: how media coverage influences strategic change. Organization Science, Vol. 24(3): 910-925.

Bertelli A. M. (2006). Motivation Crowding & the Federal Civil Servant: Evidence from the U.S. Internal Revenue Service. International Public Management Journal, Vol. 9(1): 3-23.

Bertr& M., Kramarz F., Schoar A., and Thesmar D. (2004). Politically Connected CEOs & Corporate Outcomes: Evidence from France. Unpublished Manuscript.

Bhaskaran, S. (2006). Incremental innovation and business performance: small and medium-size food enterprises in a concentrated industry environment. Journal of Small Business Management, Vol. 44(1): 64–80.

Boal, K. B., and Cummings, L. L. (1981). Cognitive evaluation theory: an experimental test of processes and outcomes. Organizational Behavior & Human Performance, Vol. 28(3): 289-310.

Boeker W. (1997). Strategic Change: The Influence of Managerial Characteristics & Organizational Growth. Academy of Management Journal, Vol. 40(1): 152.

Boivie, S., and Pollock, T. G. (2012). Time for me to fly: predicting director exit at large firms. Academy of Management Journal, Vol. 55(6): 1334.

Bologna, J. (1993). Handbook on corporate fraud. Bureau of Justice Statistics.

Bolton M. K. (1993). Imitation Versus Innovation: Lessons to be Learned from the Japanese. Organization Dynamics, Vol. 21(3): 30-45.

Bowman, E. (1982). Risk seeking by troubled firms. Sloan Management Review, Vol. 23(4): 33-42.

Boycko, M., Shleifer, A., and Vishny, R. (1995). Privatizing Russia. MIT Press.

Braithwaite, J. (1985). White collar crime. Annual Review of Sociology, Vol. 11(1): 1-25.

Brav A., Jiang W., Partnoy F., and Thomas R. (2008). Hedge Fund Activism, Corporate Governance, & Firm Performance. Journal of Finance, Vol. 63(4): 1729-1775.

Bromiley P. (1991). Testing a Causal Model of Corporate Risk Taking & Performance. Academy of Management Journal, Vol. 34(1): 37-59.

Bromiley P., Miller K. D., and Rau D. (2001). Risk in Strategic Management Research. Hitt M. A., Freeman R. E., and Harrison J. S. The Blackwell H&book of Strategic Management. Wiley, 255-283.

Brooks R. C., Riley Jr R. A., and Thomas J. (2005). Detecting & Preventing the Financing of Terrorist Activities: A Role for Government Accountants. Journal of Government Financial Management, Vol. 54(1): 12-18.

Brouthers K. D., Brouthers L. E., and Werner S. (2002). Industrial Sector, Perceived Environmental Uncertainty & Entry Mode Strategy. Journal of Business Research, Vol. 55(6): 495-507.

Burgelman, R. A. (1991). Intraorganizational ecology of strategy making and organizational adaptation: theory and field research. Organization Science, Vol. 2(3): 239-262.

Busenitz, L. W., and Lau, C. M. (1996). A cross-cultural cognitive model of new venture creation. Entrepreneurship Theory & Practice, Vol. 20.

Bushman R., Chen Q., Engel E., and Smith A. (2004). Financial Accounting Information, Organizational Complexity & Corporate Governance Systems. Journal of Accounting & Economics, Vol. 37(2): 167-201.

Cai, Chun, Li, Ming and He, Hui (2013). Restraint Condition, IPO Earnings Management and Corporate Performance——Viewpoint from Accruals and Real Earnings Management. Accounting Research, Vol. (10): 35-42.

Cai, Chun, Zhu, Rong and Xie, Liufang (2011). A Review of Research on Real Earnings Management. Economics Information, Vol. (12): 125-130.

Camerer C. F. (2004). Prospect Theory in the Wild: Evidence from the Field. Advances in Behavioral Economics, 148-161.

Carver, C. S., & Scheier, M. F. (1982). Control theory: a useful conceptual framework for personality–social, clinical, and health psychology. Psychological Bulletin, Vol. 92(1): 111-135.

Chaney, P. K., Faccio, M., & Parsley, D. (2011). The quality of accounting information in politically connected firms ☆. Journal of Accounting & Economics, Vol. 51(1): 58-76.

Charumilind, C., Kali, R., and Wiwattanakantang, Y. (2006). Connected lending: thailand before the financial crisis. Journal of Business, Vol. 79(1): 181-218.

Chen, Deqiu and Zhong, Yunjia (2011). Institutional Efficiency, Family-based Routes and Family Investment Preference. Journal of Finance and Economics, Vol. (12): 107-117.

Chen, Guohui and Zhang, Jinsong (2008). Study on the Game Theory in the Governance of Financial Fraud in Listed Companies. Research on Financial and Economic Issues, Vol. (1): 51-56.

Chen G. M., Firth M., Gao D. N., and Rui O. M. (2006). Ownership Structure, Corporate Governance, & Fraud: Evidence from China. Journal of Corporate Finance, Vol. 12(3): 424-448.

Chen, S., Sun, Z., Tang, S., and Wu, D. (2011). Government intervention and investment efficiency: evidence from china. Journal of Corporate Finance, Vol. 17(2): 259-271.

Chen T., Harford J., and Lin C. (2015). Do Analysts Matter for Governance? Evidence from Natural Experiments. Journal of Financial Economics, Vol. 115(2): 383-410.

Warfield, T. D. (2005). Equity incentives and earnings management. Accounting Review, Vol. 80(2): 441-476.

Chrisman J. J., and Patel P. C. (2012). Variations in R&D Investments of Family & Nonfamily Firms: Behavioral Agency & Myopic Loss Aversion Perspectives. Academy of Management Journal, Vol. 55(4): 976-997.

Claessens S., Feijen E., and Laeven L. (2008). Political Connections & Preferential Access to Finance: The Role of Campaign Contributions. Journal of Financial Economics, Vol. 88(3): 554-580.

Coase R. (1998). The New Institutional Economics. The American Economic Review, Vol. 88(2): 72-74.

Coleman, J. W. (1987). Toward an integrated theory of white-collar crime. American Journal of Sociology, Vol. 93(2): 406-439.

Cooke F. L., and Lin Z. (2012). Chinese Firms in Vietnam: Investment Motives, Institutional Environment & Human Resource Challenges. Asia Pacific Journal of Human Resources, Vol. 50(2): 205-226.

Courtney, J. F. (2001). Decision making and knowledge management in inquiring organizations: toward a new decision-making paradigm for dss. Decision Support Systems,Vol. 31(1): 17-38.

Cressey, D. R. (1950). The criminal violation of financial trust. American Sociological Review, Vol. 15(6): 738-743.

Crutchley, C. E., Jensen, M. R. H., and Marshall, B. B. (2007). Climate for scandal: corporate environments that contribute to accounting fraud. Financial Review, Vol. 42(1): 53–73.

Cui, A. S., Calantone, R. J., and Griffith, D. A. (2011). Strategic change and termination of interfirm partnerships. Strategic Management Journal, Vol. 32(4): 402–423.

Cull, R., and Xu, L. C. (2005). Institutions, ownership, and finance: the determinants of profit reinvestment among Chinese firms ☆. Journal of Financial Economics, Vol. 77(1): 117-146.

Cumming, D., Hou, W., and Lee, E. (2016). Business ethics and finance in greater china: synthesis and future directions in sustainability, csr, and fraud. Journal of Business Ethics, Vol. 138(4): 1-26.

Currim, I. S., Lim, J., and Kim, J. W. (2012). You get what you pay for: the effect of top executives' compensation on advertising and r&d spending decisions and stock market return. Journal of Marketing, Vol. 76(5): 33-48.

Cyert R. M., and March J. G. (1963). A Behavioral Theory of the Firm. Prentice-Hall, Englewood Cliffs, NI.

Dan, R. D., and Hitt, M. A. (2007). 1 the fundamental agency problem and its mitigation. Academy of Management Annals, Vol. 1(1): 1-64.

D'Aunno, T., and Sutton, R. I. (1992). The responses of drug abuse treatment organizations to financial adversity: a partial test of the threat-rigidity thesis. Journal of Management, Vol. 18(1): 117-131.

D'Aveni R. A. (1989). The Aftermath of Organizational Decline: A Longitudinal Study of the Strategic & Managerial Characteristics of Declining Firms. Academy of Management Journal, Vol. 32(3): 577-605.

Davidoff S. M. (2013). A Push to End Securities Fraud Lawsuits Gains Momentum. New York Times. (15 October).

Deangelo, L. E. (1981). Auditor independence, 'low balling', and disclosure regulation. Journal of Accounting & Economics, Vol. 3(2): 113-127.

Dechow, P. M., Sloan, R. G., and Sweeney, A. P. (1995). Detecting earnings management. Accounting Review, Vol. 70(2): 193-225.

Dechow P. M., Sloan R. G., and Sweeney A. P. (1996). Causes & Consequences of Earnings Manipulation: An Analysis of Firms Subject to Enforcement Actions by the SEC. Contemporary Accounting Research, Vol. 13(1): 1-36.

Deci E. L., and Ryan A. M. (2012). Self-Determination Theory. Lange P. A. M. V., Kruglanski A. W., Higgins E. T., H. Book of Theories of Social Psychology. SAGE, Los Angeles, CA.

Deci E. L., and Ryan R. M. (1985). Intrinsic Motivation & Self-Determination in Human Behavior. Plenum, New York.

Deci E. L., and Ryan R. M. (2000). The “What”&“Why” of Goal Pursuits: Human Needs & the Self-Determination of Behavior. Psychological Inquiry, Vol. 11(4): 227-268.

Devos J., Van L and eghem H., Deschoolmeester D. (2012). The Theory of the Lemon Markets in IS Research. Dwivedi Y. K., Wade M. R., Schneberger S. L., Information Systems Theory. Springer, New York, NY, 213~229.

Dewenter, K. L., and Malatesta, P. H. (2001). State-owned and privately owned firms: an empirical analysis of profitability, leverage, and labor intensity. American Economic Review, Vol. 91(1): 320-334.

Dhaliwal D. S., Radhakrishnan S., Tsang A., and Yang Y. G. (2012). Nonfinancial Disclosure & Analyst Forecast Accuracy: International Evidence on Corporate Social Responsibility Disclosure. The Accounting Review, Vol. 87(3): 723-759.

Dinan, T. G., Stilling, R. M., Stanton, C., and Cryan, J. F. (2015). Collective unconscious: how gut microbes shape human behavior. Journal of Psychiatric Research, Vol. 63(2): 1-9.

Dooley, D. V. (2002). Financial fraud: accounting theory and practice. Fordham Journal of Corporate & Financial Law, 8, S53.

Dorminey, J., Fleming, A. S., Kranacher, M. J., and Jr, R. A. R. (2012). The evolution of fraud theory. Issues in Accounting Education, Vol. 27(2): 555-579.

Du, Xingqiang, Zeng, Quan and Wu, Jiewen (2012). Practice and Experience of Officials (PEO), Economic Growth and Political Promotion – Empirical Evidence from Provincial Officials in China from 1978 to 2008. Journal of Financial Research, Vol. (2): 30-47.

Du, Xingqiang, Lei, Yu and Guo, Jianhua (2009). Political Connections, Types of Political Connections and Accounting Conservatism of Private Listed Companies. China Industrial Economics, Vol. (7): 87-97.

Dyck A. and Zingales L. (2003). The Media & Asset Prices. Working Paper. Harvard Business School.

Dyck, A., and Zingales, L. (2010). Who blows the whistle on corporate fraud?. Journal of Finance, Vol. 65(6): 2213–2253.

Eaglesham J. and Rapoport M. (2015). SEC Gets Busy with Accounting Investigations. Wall Street Journal, Vol. (1): 20.

Earley, P. C., Northcraft, G. B., Lee, C., and Lituchy, T. R. (1990). Impact of process and outcome feedback on the relation of goal setting to task performance. Academy of Management Journal, Vol. 33(1): 87-105.

Faccio, M. (2006). Politically connected firms. Social Science Electronic Publishing, Vol. 96(1): 369-386.

Fan, Gang, Wang, Xiaolu and Zhu, Hengpeng (2011). NERI INDEX of Marketization of China's Provinces 2011 Report. Economic Science Press.

Fan J. P., Wong T. J., and Zhang T. (2007). Politically Connected CEOs, Corporate Governance, & Post-IPO Performance of China's Newly Partially Privatized Firms. Journal of Financial Economics, Vol. 84(2): 330-357.

Feng, Sixian, Jiang, Fuxin and Xiao, Zelei (2012). Review and Prospect of Research on Political Connection Behavior of Enterprises. Foreign Economies and Management, Vol. (12): 63-70.

Fich, E. M., and Shivdasani, A. (2007). Financial fraud, director reputation, and shareholder wealth ☆. Journal of Financial Economics, Vol. 86(2): 306-336.

Firth, M., Lin, C., Liu, P., and Xuan, Y. (2013). The client is king: do mutual fund relationships bias analyst recommendations?. Journal of Accounting Research, Vol. 51(1): 165–200.

Fisman, R. (2001). Estimating the value of political connections. American Economic Review, Vol. 91(4): 1095-1102.

Fombrun, C. J., and Ginsberg, A. (1990). Shifting gears: enabling change in corporate aggressiveness. Strategic Management Journal, Vol. 11(4): 297-308.

Franz, D. R., Hassabelnaby, H. R., and Lobo, G. J. (2014). Impact of proximity to debt covenant violation on earnings management. Review of Accounting Studies, Vol. 19(1): 473-505.

Fung, M. K. (2015). Cumulative prospect theory and managerial incentives for fraudulent financial reporting. Contemporary Accounting Research, Vol. 32(1): 55–75.

Gagné, Marylène, and Deci, Edward L. (2005). Self-determination theory and work motivation. Journal of Organizational Behavior, Vol. 26(4): 331–362.

Gande, A., and Lewis, C. M. (2009). Shareholder-initiated class action lawsuits: shareholder wealth effects and industry spillovers. Journal of Financial & Quantitative Analysis, Vol. 44(4):. 823-850.

Geiger, M. A., and North, D. S. (2006). Does hiring a new cfo change things? an investigation of changes in discretionary accruals. Accounting Review, Vol. 81(4): 781-809.

Georgellis, Y., Iossa, E., and Tabvuma, V. (2010). Crowding out intrinsic motivation in the public sector. Journal of Public Administration Research & Theory, Vol. 21(3): 473-493(21).

Giaccotto C., Santerre R. E., and Vernon J. A. (2005). Drug Prices & Research & Development Investment Behavior in the Pharmaceutical Industry. The Journal of Law & Economics, Vol. 48(1): 195-214.

Goldman, E., Rocholl, J., and So, J. (2013). Politically connected boards of directors and the allocation of procurement contracts. Social Science Electronic Publishing, Vol. 17(5): 1617-1648.

Goranova, M., Dharwadkar, R., and Brandes, P. (2010). Owners on both sides of the deal: mergers and acquisitions and overlapping institutional ownership. Strategic Management Journal, Vol. 31(10): 1114–1135.

Greve, H. R. (1998). Performance, aspirations, and risky organizational change. Administrative Science Quarterly, Vol. 43(1): 58-86.

Greve, H. R. (2003). Investment and the behavioral theory of the firm: evidence from shipbuilding. Industrial & Corporate Change, Vol. 12(12): 1051-1076.

Greve H. R. (2003). Organizational Learning from Performance Feedback: A Behavioral Perspective on Innovation & Change. Cambridge University Press, Cambridge, UK.

Greve, H. R. (2015). Positional rigidity: low performance and resource acquisition in large and small firms. Strategic Management Journal, Vol. 32(1): 103-114.

Grinyer, P., and Mckiernan, P. (1990). Generating major change in stagnating companies. Strategic Management Journal, Vol. 11(1): 131-146.

Gross E. (2016). Development of a Financial Decision-Making Self-Efficacy Measure for Older Adults" Wayne State University, Doctoral.

Hadley, J., Zuckerman, S., and Iezzoni, L. I. (1996). Financial pressure and competition. Medical Care, Vol. 34(3): 205-219.

Harris J., and Bromiley P. (2007). Incentives to Cheat: The Influence of Executive Compensation & Firm Performance on Financial Misrepresentation. Organization Science, Vol. 18(3): 350-367.

Haynes, K. T., and Hillman, A. (2010). The effect of board capital and ceo power on strategic change. Strategic Management Journal, Vol. 31(11): 1145–1163.

Hermanson D. R., Moran B., Rossie C., and Wolfe D. (2006). Continuous Monitoring of Transactions to Reduce Fraud, Misuse, & Errors. Journal of Forensic Accounting, Vol. (7): 17-30.

Hillman, A. J., Keim, G. D., and Schuler, D. (2004). Corporate political activity: a review and research agenda. Journal of Management, Vol. 30(6): 837-857.

Hoskisson, R. E., Castleton, M. W., and Withers, M. C. (2009). Complementarity in monitoring and bonding: more intense monitoring leads to higher executive compensation. Academy of Management Perspectives, Vol. 23(2): 57-74.

Hou, W., and Moore, G. (2010). Player and referee roles held jointly: the effect of state ownership on china's regulatory enforcement against fraud. Journal of Business Ethics, Vol. 95(2): 317-335.

Huang, Xinjian, Zhang, Hui and Rao, Xi (2011). Political Connection, Audit Requirement and Quality of Accounting Information: Empirical Evidence from Chinese Listed Companies. Technology Economics, Vol. 30(4):118-121.

Huberts, L. W. J. C. (1998). What can be done against public corruption and fraud: expert views on strategies to protect public integrity. Crime Law & Social Change, Vol. 29(2-3): 209-224.

I. Serdar Dinç. (2005). Politicians and banks: political influences on government-owned banks in emerging markets ☆. Journal of Financial Economics, Vol. 77(2): 453-479.

Jacquart, P., & Armstrong, J. S. (2013). Are top executives paid enough? an evidence-based review. Social Science Electronic Publishing, Vol. 43(6): 580-589.

Jaggi B. L. (1975). The Impact of the Cultural Environment on Financial Disclosures. International Journal of Accounting, Vol. 10(2): 75-84.

Janis, I. L., and Mann, L. (1977). Emergency decision making: a theoretical analysis of responses to disaster warnings. J Human Stress, Vol. 3(2): 35.

Jensen, M. C. (1993). The modern industrial revolution, exit, and the failure of internal control systems. Journal of Finance, Vol. 48(3): 831-880.

Jia, Ming and Zhang, Zhe (2010). Does the Political Connection of High-ranking Managers Influence the Corporate Philanthropy?. Management World, Vol. (4):99-113.

Johnson, S., and Mitton, T. (2001). Cronyism and capital controls: evidence from Malaysia ☆. Journal of Financial Economics, Vol. 67(2): 351-382.

Johnson, W. B., Magee, R. P., Nagarajan, N. J., and Newman, H. A. (2016). An analysis of the stock price reaction to sudden executive deaths ☆: implications for the managerial labor market. Journal of Accounting & Economics, Vol. 7(1): 151-174.

Kaa, E. J. V. D. (2010). Prospect theory and choice behavior strategies: review and synthesis of concepts from social and transport sciences. European Journal of Transport & Infrastructure Research, Vol. 10(4): 299-329.

Kahneman D, and Tversky A. (1979). Prospect Theory: An Analysis of Decision under Risk. Econometrica: Journal of the Econometric Society, 263-291.

Kang, E. (2008). Director interlocks and spillover effects of reputational penalties from fraudulent financial reporting. Academy of Management Journal, Vol. 51(3): 537-555.

Kassem R., and Higson A. (2012). The New Fraud Triangle Model. Journal of Emerging Trends in Economics & Management Sciences, Vol. 191-195(3).

Katz D. and Kahn R. L. (1978). The Social Psychology of Organizations (Vol. 2). Wiley.

Kelley C. M .(1976). Accountants & Auditors vs. White Collar Crime. The Internal Auditor, Vol. 33(3): 35-39.

Khwaja, A. I., and Mian, A. (2005). Do lenders favor politically connected firms? rent provision in an emerging financial market. Quarterly Journal of Economics, Vol.120(4): 1371-1411.

King, B. L. (2008). Strategizing at leading venture capital firms: of planning, opportunism and deliberate emergence. Long Range Planning, Vol. 41(3): 345-366.

Kirton, M. (1976). Adaptors and innovators: a description and measure. Journal of Applied Psychology, Vol. 61(5): 622-629.

Kong, Chen and Yu, Hongjian (2015). The Formation Mechanism of Accounting Fraud: Research Perspective and Future Prospect. Journal of Dongbei University of Finance and Economics, Vol. (1):18-25.

Kőszegi B., and Rabin M. (2006). A Model of Reference-Dependent Preferences. The Quarterly Journal of Economics, Vol. 121(4): 1133-1165.

Kőszegi, B., and Rabin, M. (2007). Reference-dependent risk attitudes. American Economic Review, Vol. 97(4): 1047-1073.

Kőszegi B. and Rabin M. (2009). Reference-dependent Consumption Plans. The American Economic Review, Vol. 99(3): 909-936.

Krueger, A. O. (1974). The political economy of the rent-seeking society. American Economic Review, Vol. 64(3): 291-303.

Kumar, S., and Goyal, N. (2015). Behavioral biases in investment decision making – a systematic literature review. Qualitative Research in Financial Markets, Vol. 7(1): 88-108.

La Porta R., Lopez-de-Silanes F., Shleifer A., and Vishny R. (1999). The Quality of Government. The Journal of Law, Economics, & Organization, Vol. 15(1): 222-279.

Lemmon, M. L., and Lins, K. V. (2003). Ownership structure, corporate governance, and firm value: evidence from the east Asian financial crisis. Journal of Finance, Vol. 58(4): 1445-1468.

Leuz, C., and Oberholzer-Gee, F. (2006). Political relationships, global financing, and corporate transparency: evidence from Indonesia ☆. Journal of Financial Economics, Vol. 81(2): 411-439.

Li H. and Atuahene-Gima K. (2001). Product Innovation Strategy & the Performance of New Technology Ventures in China", Academy of Management Journal, Vol. 44(6): 1123-1134.

Li, H., and Zhang, Y. (2007). The role of managers' political networking and functional experience in new venture performance: evidence from china's transition economy. Strategic Management Journal, Vol. 28(8): 791-804.

Li, K., and Zhao, X. (2008). Asymmetric information and dividend policy. Financial Management, Vol. 37(4): 673–694.

Li, S., Selover, D. D., and Stein, M. (2011). “keep silent and make money”: institutional patterns of earnings management in china. Journal of Asian Economics, Vol. 22(5): 369-382.

Lian, Yanling, He, Xiaogang and Gao, Hao (2014). The Performance Aspiration Gap and the Strategy Adjustment: A Case Study Based on China’s Listed Companies. Management World, Vol. (11):119-132.

Lian, Yanling, Zhou, Bing and Liu, Junliang (2016). Compliance or Violation? Risk Decision Analysis under Expectation Gap: A Case Study of Listed Companies in China. Quarterly Journal of Management, Vol. (z1):47-72.

Lin, C., Lin, P., Song, F. M., and Li, C. (2011). Managerial incentives, ceo characteristics and corporate innovation in china’s private sector. Journal of Comparative Economics, Vol. 39(2): 176-190.

Liu, Huilong, Zhang, Min, Wang, Yaping and Wu, Liansheng (2010). Political Connections, Compensation Incentive and Employee Allocation Efficiency. Economic Research Journal, Vol. (9):134-138.

Liu, Xiaofei (2016). New pattern of A-share companies in 2016: The number of companies exceeded 3,000 for the first time and reached a new high of over a trillion Yuan. http://finance.china.com.cn/.

Liu, Xiaoxuan (2003). The Structure of Property Rights in the Chinese Transition Economy. Economic Research Journal, Vol. (1):21-29.

Liu, Yunsheng (2011). Research on Financial Maturity of Guangdong. Economic Science Press.

Lu, Taiping and Zhang, Dongxu (2014). Financing Demand, Financing Constraints and Earnings Management. Accounting Research, Vol. (1):35-41.

Luo, Danglun and Liu, Xiaolong (2009). Political Relationship, Barriers to Entry and Enterprise Performance – the evidences from the privately listed enterprises. Management World, Vol. (5):97-106.

Luo, Danglun and Tang, Qingquan (2009). The Performance of Institutional Environment Evidence from China's Private Listed Companies. Economic Research Journal, Vol. (2):106-118.

March J. G. (1991). Exploration & Exploitation in Organizational Learning. Organization Science, Vol. 2(1): 71-87.

March J. G. and Simon H. A. (1958). Organizations. Wiley, New York.

Markóczy, L. (2001). Consensus formation during strategic change. Strategic Management Journal, Vol. 22(11): 1013-1031.

Mcgrath, R. G., & Nerkar, A. (2004). Real options reasoning and a new look at the r&d investment strategies of pharmaceutical firms. Strategic Management Journal, Vol. 25(1): 1-21.

Messner S. F. and Rosenfeld R. (2012). Crime & the American Dream. Cengage Learning.

Meyer A., Goes J., and Brooks G. (1993). Organizational Change & Redesign. Longitudinal Field Research Methods: Studying Processes in Organizational Change, 66-111.

Miller, D., and Friesen, P. H. (1983). Strategy-making and environment: the third link. Strategic Management Journal, Vol. 4(3): 221-235.

Modigliani F. and Miller M. H. (1958). The Cost of Capital, Corporation Finance & the Theory of Investment. American Economic Review, Vol. 48(3): 261-297.

North D. C. (1990). Institutions, Institutional Change, & Economic Performance. Cambridge University Press.

North D. C. and Thomas R. P. (1973). The Rise of the Western World: A New Economic History. Cambridge University Press, UK.

O'Gara, J. D. (2004). Corporate fraud: Incident studies in detection and prevention.

Oliver, C. (1992). The antecedents of deinstitutionalization. Organization Studies, Vol. 13(4): 563-588.

Osterloh, M., and Frey, B. S. (2000). Motivation, knowledge transfer, and organizational forms. Organization Science, Vol. 11(5): 538-550.

Margit Osterloh, Jetta Frost, and Bruno S. Frey. (2002). The dynamics of motivation in new organizational forms. International Journal of the Economics of Business, Vol. 9(1): 61-77.

Peng M. W. and Heath P. S. (1996). The Growth of the Firm in Planned Economies in Transition: Institutions, Organizations, & Strategic Choice. Academy of Management Review, Vol. 21(2): 492-528.

Pepper, A., and Gore, J. (2012). Behavioral agency theory: new foundations for theorizing about executive compensation. Lse Research Online Documents on Economics, Vol. 41(4): 1045-1068.

Phillips, J. S., and Lord, R. G. (1981). Causal attributions and perceptions of leadership. Organizational Behavior & Human Performance, Vol. 28(2): 143-163.

Pollet, J. M., and Wilson, M. (2008). How does size affect mutual fund behavior?. Journal of Finance, Vol. 63(6): 2941–2969.

Porta R. L., Lopez-de-Silanes F., Shleifer A., and Vishny R. W. (1998). Law & Finance. Journal of Political Economy, Vol. 106(6): 1113~1155.

Porter M. E. (1992). Capital Choices: Changing the Way America Invests in Industry. Harvard Business School Press, Boston, MA.

Pryor, B. D., Bologna, S. G., and Kahl, L. E. (2010). Risk factors for serious infection during treatment with cyclophosphamide and high-dose corticosteroids for systemic lupus erythematosus. Arthritis & Rheumatism, Vol. 39(9): 1475-1482.

Qi, Xuan, Gu, Huili and Liu, Shuhai (2013). Regional Factors Influencing the Voluntary Accounting Information Disclosure of Listed Companies——From the Perspective of Financing Constraints. Journal of Yunnan University of Finance and Economics, Vol. (2).

Qian, Yingyi, and Weingas, Barry R. (1996). China's transition to markets: market-preserving federalism, Chinese style. Journal of Economic Policy Reform, Vol. 1(2): 149-185.

Qin, Jiangping and Duan, Xingmin (2005). Game Analysis of Accounting Fraud and Its Supervision in Enterprise. On Economic Problems, Vol. (8):73-75.

Rao, Xi (2012). Political Connection, Accounting Quality and Firms' Investment Efficiency. Chongqing University.

Rao, Yancho and Hu, Yiming. A Study on the Survey of the Accounting Information Used by the Bank Lenders. Accounting Research, Vol. (4):38-43+96-97.

Reinstein A. and Bayou M. E. (1998). The New Auditing Standard on Fraud can Help Financial Institutions", Journal of Lending & Credit Risk Management, Vol. 80(8): 58-63.

Rezaee Z. (2002). Fraudulent financial reporting: Prevention & Detection. John Wiley & Sons, NJ.

Roberts, B. E. (1990). Political institutions, policy expectations, and the 1980 election: a financial market perspective. American Journal of Political Science, Vol. 34(2): 289-310.

Robinson, S. N., Robertson, J. C., and Curtis, M. B. (2012). The effects of contextual and wrongdoing attributes on organizational employees' whistleblowing intentions following fraud. Journal of Business Ethics, Vol. 106(2): 213-227.

Roodposhti, F. R., and Chashmi, S. A. N. (2011). The impact of corporate governance mechanisms on earnings management. African Journal of Business Management, Vol. 5(11): 4143-4151.

Ross, L., and Ward, A. (1995). Psychological barriers to dispute resolution. Advances in Experimental Social Psychology, Vol. 27(08): 255-304.

Ryan R. M. and Deci E. L. (2000). Self-Determination Theory & the Facilitation of Intrinsic Motivation, Social Development, & Well-Being. American Psychologist, Vol. 55(1): 68-78.

Schmidt, U., Starmer, C., and Sugden, R. (2008). Third-generation prospect theory. Journal of Risk & Uncertainty, Vol. 36(3): 203-223.

Shi W., Connelly B. L., and Hoskisson R. E. (2016). External corporate governance & financial fraud: cognitive evaluation theory insights on agency theory prescriptions. Strategic Management Journal.

Shi W., Connelly B. L., and Sanders W. G. (2016). Buying Bad Behavior: Tournament Incentives & Securities Class Action Lawsuits. Strategic Management Journal, Vol. 37(7): 1354-1378.

Shin, Y., Sun, Y. S., Jin, N. C., and Min, S. K. (2015). Top management ethical leadership and firm performance: mediating role of ethical and procedural justice climate. Journal of Business Ethics, Vol. 129(1): 43-57.

Shleifer A. and Vishny R. (1998). The Grabbing Hand. Harvard University Press, Cambridge.

Sonenshein, S., and Dholakia, U. (2012). Explaining employee engagement with strategic change implementation: a meaning-making approach. Organization Science, Vol. 23(1): 1-23.

Stein, J. C. (1989). Efficient capital markets, inefficient firms: a model of myopic corporate behavior. Quarterly Journal of Economics, Vol. 104(4): 655-669.

Stone D. N., Deci E. L., and Ryan R. M. (2009). Beyond Talk: Creating Autonomous Motivation through Self-Determination Theory. Journal of General Management, Vol. 34(3): 75-91.2

Chamu Sundaramurthy, and Marianne Lewis. (2003). Control and collaboration: paradoxes of governance. Academy of Management Review, Vol. 28(3): 397-415.

Tan, J., and Tan, D. (2005). Environment–strategy co-evolution and co-alignment: a staged model of Chinese soes under transition. Strategic Management Journal, Vol. 26(2): 141-157.

Tang, Song and Sun, Zheng (2014). Political Connection, Executive Compensation and Future Business Performance. Management World, Vol. (5):93-105.

Tang, Z., and Hull, C. (2012). An investigation of entrepreneurial orientation, perceived environmental hostility, and strategy application among Chinese smes. Journal of Small Business Management, Vol. 50(1): 132–158.

Troy, C., Smith, K. G., and Domino, M. A. (2011). Ceo demographics and accounting fraud: who is more likely to rationalize illegal acts?. Strategic Organization, Vol. 9(4): 259-282.

Tunley M. (2011). Uncovering the Iceberg: Mandating the measurement of fraud in the United Kingdom. International Journal of Law, Crime & Justice, Vol. 39(3): 190-203.

UzunHatice, Szewczyksamuel, H., and VarmaRaj. (2004). Board composition and corporate fraud. Financial Analysts Journal, Vol. 60(3): 33-43.

Valipour H. and Moradbeygi M. (2011). Corporate Debt Financing & Earnings Quality. Journal of Applied Finance & Banking, Vol. 3(1): 139-157.

Wang, Guo (2014). A Study on the Violations of Listed Companies in China: 1992-2011. Southwest University of Finance and Economics.

Wang, Junqiu and Ni, Chunhui (2012). Political Connections, Accounting Information and the Cost of Bank Loan——Empirical Evidence Based on China Private Listed Firms. Research on Economics and Management, Vol. (8):30-38.

Wang, Kemin and Liu, Bo (2012). Performance Threshold and Earnings Management of Public Offering. Management World, 2012(8):30-42.

Wang, Mingli (2012). Monetary Policy, Corporate Governance and Earnings Management. Commercial Research, Vol. (2):55-64.

Wang, Qingwen and Wu, Shinong (2008). The Impact of Political Relations on Corporate Performance: A Case Study Based on the Political Impact Index of Listed Companies in China. International Symposium on Accounting Research in China.

Wee, G. P. V. (2010). Prospect theory and travel behavior: a personal reflection based on a seminar. European Journal of Transport & Infrastructure Research, Vol. 10(4): 385-394.

Wiersema, M. F., and Zhang, Y. (2011). Ceo dismissal: the role of investment analysts. Strategic Management Journal, Vol. 32(11): 1161-1182.

Wilks T. J. and Zimbelman M. F. (2004). Using Game Theory & Strategic Reasoning Concepts to Prevent & Detect Fraud. Accounting Horizons, Vol. 18(3): 173-184.

Williamson O. and Ouchi W. (1981). The Market & Heirarchies Perspective: Origins, Implications, Prospects. Assessing Organizational Design & Performance. Wiley, New York.

Wiseman, R. M., and Gomezmejia, L. R. (1998). A behavioral agency model of managerial risk taking. Academy of Management Review, Vol. 23(1): 133-153.

Wu, Jinglian and Huang, Shaoqing (2007). Innovation or Rent-seeking: Institutional Environment and Entrepreneurial Behavior in the Transition Period in China. Journal of Legal and Economic Studies, Vol. (7).

Wu, Wenfeng, Wu, Chongfeng and Liu, Xiaowei (2008). Political Connection and Market Valuation: Evidence from China Individual-controlled Listed Firms (2008). Economic Research Journal, Vol. (7):130-141.

Wu,Wenfeng, Wu, Chongfeng and Rui, Meng (2009). Between the Special Connections that High-ranking Managers of Some of China's Listed Companies Have with the Government and Tax Preference Afforded to them. Management World, Vol. (3):134-142.

Xu, Chaohui and Zhou, Zongfang (2016). Effects of Corporate Credit Risk on the Earnings Management Driven by Financing Demand. Management Review, Vol. 28(7):12-21.

Xu, Nianhang, Jiang, Xuanyu, Yi, Zhihong and Xu, Xinzhong (2012). Conflicts of Interest, Analyst Optimism and Stock Price Crash Risk. Economic Research Journal, Vol. (7):127-140.

Yan, Ting (2011). The Effects of Institutional Environment on Enforcement of Accounting Standards. Dongbei University of Finance and Economics.

Yang, Qingxiang, Yu, Lin and Chen, Na (2009). Board Characters and Financial Fraud: Empirical Evidence from Chinese Listed Companies. Accounting Research, Vol. (7):64-70.

Yu, Minggui, Hui, Yafu and Pan, Hongbo (2010). Political Connections, Rent Seeking, and the Fiscal Subsidy Efficiency of Local Governments. Economic Research Journal, Vol. (3):65-77.

Yu, Minggui and Pan, Hongbo (2008). The Relationship between Politics, Institutional Environments and Private Enterprises' Access to Bank Loans. Management World, Vol. (8):9-21.

Zahra, S. A., Priem, R. L., and Rasheed, A. A. (2005). The antecedents and consequences of top management fraud. Journal of Management, Vol. 31(6): 803-828.

Zhang, Y., and Gimeno, J. (2016). Earnings pressure and long-term corporate governance: : can long-term-oriented investors and managers reduce the quarterly earnings obsession?. Organization Science, Vol. 27(2): 354-372.

Zhang, Min and Huang, Jicheng (2009). Political Connections, Diversification and Firm's Risks: Empirical Evidence from China's Securities Market. Management World, Vol. (7):156-164.

Zhang, Sanbao and Zhang, Zhixue (2012). Regional Institutions Disparity, CEO Managerial Discretion and Firm Risk Taking: Evidence from China High-tech Firms across 30 Provinces. Management World, Vol. (4):101-114.

Zhao, Jingwen and Xu, Yuyu (2012). The Unification of the Tax Rates for Foreign and Domestic Enterprises, Tax Planning and the Choice of Earnings Management Methods. Journal of Finance and Economics, Vol. (1):135-144.

Dictionary Editorial Office, Institute of Linguistics, Chinese Academy of Social Sciences (2003). Modern Chinese Dictionary, The Commercial Press.

Zhou, Linbin and Li, Shenglan (2003). The Think of Protecting Property-right of Private Enterprises with Law in China: A View of Law and Economics. Research of Institutional Economics, Vol. (2).

Zhou, Yuanyuan, Zhuang, Minglai and Wang, Yuanhua (2011). ERP System Implement, Institutional Environment and Accounting Information Quality: Empirical Evidence from Chinese Listed Companies. Journal of Zhongnan University of Economics and Law, Vol. (3):99-106.

Zhou, Zejiang (2012). Tax Burden and Behavior of Enterprises' Earnings Management – Empirical Evidence from Chinese Listed Companies. Journal of Shanxi University of Finance and Economics, Vol. (10): 88-96.

Index

P

Q

R

S

T

U

V

W

X

Y

Z

About the Author

Dr. Peng Jinqian was born on June 19th, 1976 in Luhe County, Guangdong Province. He earned his Ph. D. of Business Administration from Hong Kong Polytechnic University. He started his career as a professional advisor for business in 2000 and is currently the standing committee member of the Political Consultative Conference of Luhe County, Guangdong Province, the chairman of Lin Run Group Co., Ltd., the director of the Rural Commercial Bank of Luhe County, Guangdong Province, and the general manager of Guangdong Baili Food Co., Ltd.

Made in United States
Orlando, FL
04 November 2026

90204698R00116